THE
ENTERTAINING
BIBLE

Publications International, Ltd.

Favorite Brand Name Recipes at www.fbnr.com

Photography on pages 5, 8, 9, 13, 16, 17, 18, 23 (upper left), 26, 30, 31 and 33 by Proffitt Photography, Ltd., Chicago.

Pictured on the front cover *(counterclockwise from top left):* Mediterranean Vegetable Bake *(page 202),* Triple Chocolate Cake *(page 302)* and Double Cheese Veal Cutlets *(page 72).*

Pictured on the back cover *(left to right):* Turkey with Pecan-Cherry Stuffing *(page 94)* and Rosemary-Scented Nut Mix *(page 38).*

ISBN: 1-4127-2172-5

Library of Congress Control Number: 2004118179

Manufactured in China.

8 7 6 5 4 3 2 1

Microwave Cooking: Microwave ovens vary in wattage. Use the cooking times as guidelines and check for doneness before adding more time.

Preparation/Cooking Times: Preparation times are based on the approximate amount of time required to assemble the recipe before cooking, baking, chilling or serving. These times include preparation steps such as measuring, chopping and mixing. The fact that some preparations and cooking can be done simultaneously is taken into account. Preparation of optional ingredients and serving suggestions is not included.

contents

Entertaining Fundamentals

Do you get nervous at the thought of having friends over for appetizers and drinks? Are you frazzled when your family comes for dinner? Would you like to host a party but don't know where to begin? Then this book is for you—and every other first-time party giver, nervous cook and can't-seem-to-get-it-right host.

The Entertaining Bible will not teach you how to plan an elaborate wedding reception, a formal gourmet dinner party or a buffet for 200. Instead, it will give you the tools and guidance you need to host an informal dinner party for 12, an open house for 30 or an afternoon tea for your 6 closest friends. When you've mastered the basics, if you'd like, you can move on to tackle those bigger and more elaborate challenges.

The most important key to successful entertaining is planning. If you think those fabulous parties and dinners you've attended came together quickly and easily, you're wrong. The best hosts have carefully planned every detail—from invitations and menus to table settings, decorations and wine. The second key is practice. Just like anything you want to master, the more you practice, the easier it gets and the

better job you do. With the help of this book, you can learn how to organize all the details that make for a great get-together. And with practice, you'll be just as great a party-giver as those hosts you admire.

In the pages that follow you'll find tips, ideas and inspiration for effortless entertaining. A selection of more than 180 sure-to-please recipes are included. Plus, there are sample menus for a variety of occasions that will get you on your way to giving a party that everyone will love.

Party Planning

Begin at the beginning: The best place to start is with a reason to get people together. A desire to celebrate is a favorite motive. Birthdays, anniversaries, graduations, promotions, engagements or new babies are all great reasons. And what better way is there to wish someone well than with a special dinner or festive party? With the exception of kids' parties, no activities need to be planned unless you wish to. Good food, conversation and gift-giving are the basic goals.

A traditional way to observe a

holiday is with a gathering of family and friends. Long-standing traditions often dictate the menu and activities, but give some thought to adding new items to the menu or starting a new holiday custom. Make only a few small changes if you think your family may resist anything new. For instance, you can ease them toward a more meaningful celebration, an easier-to prepare menu or healthier dishes.

Maybe you just want to get friends together to catch up, introduce your new boyfriend, say goodbye to friends moving to Borneo, or to thank someone for a kindness. You can also plan a party around an event, such as the Super Bowl or the Academy Awards.

Another goal is to host a meeting or get people together to accomplish a task, which is easier and more fun with a group of friends. You might want to host a book club or PTA committee meeting, plan a Christmas cookie baking day or help a friend with a broken leg get household chores done.

Finally, there are times when the best reason is no reason—a spur-of-the-moment get-together. If you have only a day (or an hour) for planning, there are several ways to manage this (see page 21).

Advance Planning

Now that you know why you want to entertain, it's time to decide how to do it. Here are some things to consider before you get too deeply into planning:

Number of guests: Get a rough idea of how many people you want to invite. As the number increases so does the cost and the time needed for organizing and preparing for the occasion. Keep in mind the size of your home. Not every house can accommodate 30 guests. Nor can every kitchen turn out a meal for a large number of people. If you've never entertained, plan to start on a small scale with just a handful of guests and simple dishes; when you've gained some confidence, you can think about entertaining your entire family or plan a more elaborate get-together.

Stand up or sit down: If you want to have a sit-down dinner, keep the guest list in line with the number of people the dining table can seat. For larger groups, consider a buffet or an outdoor party. Even with a buffet, it's important to have enough seating for everyone. (If finding enough seating is a problem, consider an appetizer buffet with all finger food, which will be easy to eat standing up.) Folding chairs can be rented. If the gathering is very casual and the guests young, sitting on the floor is an option. Or, you can ask close friends to bring folding chairs.

Choose a date and time: Choose a date and time that will work for all your guests—you don't want to plan a party and have no one show up. If you're planning a sit-down dinner, invite people to come about 45 minutes to 1 hour before you plan to serve dinner. Buffets can be set up and ready when your guests arrive.

Meal or snack: How much you serve is often tied to the time of day of your party. If you're celebrating a family birthday on a Saturday afternoon, all you may need is a cake and beverages. However, if you invite guests for a 5:00 or 6:00 party, they will expect dinner unless the invitation indicates that you will be serving only appetizers. Guests will then know what to expect and make plans accordingly.

Invitations by mail or phone: A good rule of thumb is that the fancier the occasion, the fancier the invitation. For a special occasion such as an engagement party or a fiftieth wedding anniversary, plan to send written invitations four to six weeks in advance to make sure most people will be available. It's best to send a written invitation—they may be handwritten,

purchased (just fill in the pertinent information), or designed on the computer. For other occasions, you may choose to call family and friends instead of sending written invitations. Just make sure you give them all the necessary information—it's easy to forget something. If you know that everyone has e-mail and checks it regularly, this is another option. Except for spur-of-the-moment get-togethers, two to three weeks in advance should be adequate notice.

Always include the important information: the reason for the get-together, date, time and place. Don't forget to ask them to R.S.V.P. by a certain date. Feel free to call them if they don't respond by that date. When the party involves gift-giving, be prepared with suggestions if people ask for them.

Surprise parties: Surprise parties can be a lot of fun or a major disaster! Never surprise anyone unless you know they would enjoy it. Start planning early because it takes special care to plan the party and keep it a secret from the guest of honor. Surprising someone takes attention to detail and the help of someone who is close to the guest of honor.

Choices! Choices!

Now it's time to discuss options. Dinner buffet, appetizer buffet, sit-down dinner, barbecue, afternoon tea, theme party or open house—the choices may seem overwhelming, but really your guest list will help make the decision easy. If you've decided on 20 adult guests, then a buffet is a good way to go. If it's summer, a barbecue might work especially if children are included. A sit down dinner is ideal for a small congenial group; keep in mind that it takes planning to get food prepared and served without being absent from the table for more than a few minutes.

Buffets

This option can be done casually, but a buffet also provides the opportunity for a fancier approach. Fancy doesn't have to mean formal; however, it does give you the opportunity to pull out the good china or an excuse to buy those fantastic plates you saw on sale at the mall. You can use the silver service or stainless steel tableware or you can mix the two if you need to. Casual doesn't have to mean paper plates, plastic forks and paper napkins, but if that works for you, be sure to buy attractive, sturdy, plastic-coated plates

Should you set up a bar

When you serve alcohol at a party, keep it simple. You don't need a full bar that offers mixed drinks, beer and wine, although you may want to offer more choices for an appetizer or cocktail party. The time and expense it would take to include every one of your guests' favorite beverages may be better spent in other ways. For a cocktail party, consider limiting the selection to a couple of popular mixed drinks, like martinis. When combined with wine and beer, most everyone will find something to their liking.

You can limit choices to just wine and beer. Select one red and one white wine and buy multiple bottles of each. See "Pairing wine with food" on page 14 for more information on selecting wine. Select one or two beers: choose a domestic and an imported product. Always choose good quality wine and beer and something that you like because you'll be left with the extras.

When serving alcohol, always make sure that there is a selection of nonalcoholic beverages as well. Water and soft drinks can be augmented by juice, punch and iced tea, if you wish.

and sturdy forks and spoons. Hosts that entertain a lot sometimes keep a stock of simple inexpensive white ceramic or glass plates, mugs and glasses to mix and match with other tableware; garage sales are a good place to find these items. Or, look for inexpensive plastic or melamine tableware with trendy designs.

Full-Meal Buffets: If you choose to serve a full meal buffet style, plan to serve appetizers as the guests arrive and bring out the hot dishes about 45 minutes later. The appetizers are best placed in the living room or family room away from the main buffet table. This keeps guests busy eating and talking while you quickly add the hot foods to the already assembled room temperature and cold foods. While

guests are enjoying their meal, take a few minutes to set up dessert and coffee. It's a good idea to plan a separate small table or an out-of-the way counter for dessert.

Brunch Buffets: A brunch seems to turn an ordinary day into something special—there's an almost elegant feel to even a casual weekend brunch. What you serve at a brunch depends a little on what time you schedule it. Beginning at 11:00 or 12:00 allows you the freedom to serve breakfast or luncheon dishes or a mix of both. For a mid-morning start, breakfast food seems to work best. One of the benefits of brunch entertaining is that the menu can be kept simple and thus easy to prepare. Many hosts prepare a main

Appetizer Buffet

Rosemary-Scented Nut Mix

Festive Franks

Mini-Marinated Beef Skewers

Ham Spirals

Golden Artichoke Dip with vegetables

Pepper and Parsley Logs with crackers

Caponata with toasted bread

chips and salsa

dish and purchase cut-up fruit and bakery items; this frees the host to leisurely set up the buffet, organize the beverages and enjoy the party.

Appetizer Buffets: Appetizer buffets are another choice to consider. They work well if you provide enough food to satisfy those with good appetites. Or, schedule drinks and appetizers to precede dinner at a restaurant. If the group is going off together to a theater performance, you might want to make an evening of it and ask everyone back for dessert and coffee afterward.

Dessert Buffets: This decadent approach to entertaining can be difficult to schedule around busy lives. It probably works best as a follow-up to another activity—gather guests after an evening at a local community program, Fourth of July fireworks or a political rally; just be sure to issue invitations early enough so guests can make necessary arrangements to attend. It's a rare person who doesn't love an opportunity to try a variety of desserts, so this is a sure way to impress everyone. With a mix of bakery items and homemade treats (all made ahead), this buffet is fairly easy to put together. To round out the selection, add a wheel of cheese and several varieties of seedless grapes. Always cut tarts, cakes, brownies and pies into small servings so guests can taste an

Food Safety

On a buffet table or at a picnic, always keep hot foods hot (above 140°F) and cold foods cold (below 40°F). Use chafing dishes, hot trays or slow cookers to keep food hot. Replenish food often, avoiding adding fresh food to a dish that has been on the buffet table for a while. It is better to remove the used dish and replace it with a new dish with freshly made food. For an open house make multiples of everything. Slip a second casserole into the oven soon after guests begin arriving. Have a second salad and additional appetizers stored in the refrigerator.

Do not let cooked food stand longer than 2 hours. Any food that has remained unrefrigerated for more than 2 hours should be discarded.

How much food do you need?

It can be difficult to estimate accurately how much food you will need for any occasion. Consider what you know about your guests. Are they big eaters, dainty eaters or a mix of both? The more dishes you provide at a buffet the less of each you will need.

Per person

Appetizers

Before Dinner	4 to 6 servings
Appetizer Buffet	8 to 10 servings

Meat, Poultry, Fish

Boneless, uncooked	5 to 6 ounces
Bone-in, uncooked	6 to 8 ounces

Casserole — 1 to 1½ cups

Pasta and Sauce — 1 to 1½ cups

Sides

Pasta or Rice	½ cup
Vegetables/Fruit	½ to ⅔ cup

Salads

Greens	1 to 1¼ cups
With vegetables	¾ cup
Pasta/rice salad	½ to ⅔ cup

Soups

Appetizer	½ cup
Main Dish	1 to 1½ cups

Desserts

After Dinner	1 to 1½ servings
Dessert Buffet	6 to 8 small servings

assortment of desserts. An evening dessert party may not be the best occasion to invite children; parents probably won't appreciate kids with a late-night sugar buzz!

Where to put the buffet table: You can use your dining table or a folding table as the buffet table. Move the chairs away from the dining table (into another room if the dining room is small). Consider moving the table close to a wall to allow more room for guests to move around as they fill their plates. If possible, leave enough space for you to access the table from behind if you anticipate a need to replenish food. For those lucky enough to have a large room, you can position the table so people can serve themselves from either side; this works well when the group is large. The only problem is that guests may not be able to reach all the food; to solve this problem, do a duplicate arrangement on each side of the table.

Setting up the buffet table: Decide what would be the best direction to move guests along the buffet—right to left or left to right. Pretend you're a guest and walk through an imaginary buffet line, keeping in mind that there may be many others filling plates with food at the same time. Position a stack of plates where you want guests to begin. Use full-size plates for a full-meal buffet and salad/luncheon-sized plates for an appetizer, dessert or brunch party. If a dish such as soup or chili requires a small bowl rather than a plate, have a stack of bowls where they will be needed. Silverware and napkins are best placed at the end of the line so guests don't have to juggle them as they fill their plates; wrap the silverware in a cloth napkin and tie it with ribbon or raffia for an easy-to-carry bundle. Beverages are best located away from the buffet table in a less congested area. When you serve three courses, don't put them all on the main buffet table. Instead, plan separate tables for the appetizers and the desserts. (See "Full-Meal Buffets" on page 10.)

Attractive presentation: It is not difficult to make a buffet presentation attractive, if you know a few tricks. First, cover the table with a tablecloth (to protect your dining table or to cover an unsightly folding table). You can also buy a piece of fabric to cover the table; hem the edges (or cut them with pinking shears) or press under the raw

edges with an iron. Better yet, add a colorful runner or piece of fabric over the tablecloth to add interest. With a glass table top, cover all or part of it with a runner, cloth napkins, placemats or a tablecloth.

When all the food is placed directly on the table at the same level, the presentation will lack interest. Raise some food above the table; a couple of pedestal plates placed at the back of the table is the simplest way to to do this. Or, create a few platforms using sturdy boxes; just drape them with fabric or small tablecloths.

All the serving dishes do not need to match, but they should complement each other. Usually white or glass pieces work with colors or patterns. Or, an unattractive plate can be hidden with fresh spinach or arugula leaves, then used to serve cold sliced meat or shrimp. This is your opportunity to get creative! Rental stores offer basic serving plates that can augment your pieces.

Pairing Wine with Food

Food	Wine
Asian and spicy food	Gewurztraminer
Beef, Lamb	Cabernet Sauvignon, Chianti, Merlot, red Bordeaux, Zinfandel
Chicken, Pork, Veal	Beaujolis, Chardonnay, Pinot Grigio, Riesling, white Rhone
Fish, lean	Chardonnay, white Burgundy
Fish, moderate and high fat	Chardonnay, Pinot Noir, Sauvignon Blanc, white Burgundy, white Zinfandel
Pasta with tomato sauce	Chianti, Zinfandel
Pasta with vegetables	Riesling, Sauvignon Blanc, Valpolicella
Pasta with white sauce	Chardonnay, Pinot Grigio
Shellfish	Chablis, Chardonnay, Macon Blanc, Sauvignon Blanc

Leave room on the buffet table for decorations. A flower arrangement always works well; just be sure the arrangement has some height to it and is placed at the back of the table. Avoid heavily scented flowers, such as lilies, lilacs or peonies; they can interfere with the taste of the food. (See pages 30 to 31 for some easy decorating ideas.)

Informal Dinner Party

To some hosts, the words dinner party strike fear in their hearts. Although a dinner party seems to suggest a formal, elegant affair, it doesn't have to be. Actually, all it is is a sit-down dinner that's just a notch above a family dinner. It can be served family style with everyone serving themselves or the food can be plated in the kitchen. The differences are that you invite congenial guests (not your two cousins who argue all the time), use your best tableware, add a fabulous centerpiece and maybe serve wine. The food doesn't have to be fancy either unless you want it to be.

If you want a fancier dinner party, you can enlist the help of a caterer or hire a teenager with cooking or waitress experience to serve the food you've prepared and tend to things in the kitchen.

Selecting wine for dinner: If you choose to serve wine, the important question of what to serve becomes a dilemma. The often-heard rule of serving white wine with fish and chicken and red wine with meat certainly has some merit, but there are exceptions and the rule fails to mention meatless dishes. Some fish, such as salmon, pair well with lighter red wines while an assertive white wine can hold its own with some meat. (See the chart on page 14 for additional guidelines.) Sweeter wines require careful partnering with food. The sweetest wines are best served after dinner rather than with the main course. When pairing a sweet wine with a dessert, the wine should be sweeter than the dessert or the flavor of the wine will be lost.

Always select the wine after the menu has been chosen. Ask a knowledgeable wine store clerk or a friend for guidance. Most importantly, buy one bottle and taste it with the entrée and any flavorful side dishes in a practice run. When you're satisfied that you've made a successful pairing, purchase enough wine for the party.

Kids at Dinner Parties?

Many parents feel that children never belong at a nonfamily dinner party. But others feel strongly that including one or all of your children occasionally when you entertain informally teaches them how to behave in adult company and gives them the opportunity to practice their table manners. If your child can behave at a family dinner, consider including her/him at an adult dinner party. Interested children can play a role in planning a dinner, setting the table or clearing the dishes while you get the dessert and coffee.

Barbecues or Picnics: For someone who has never entertained, barbecues are a good place to start— they're so casual, everyone is willing to help and the food is uncomplicated. All you need is a backyard (or a park), a grill, a table and food. Here paper plates, paper napkins and plastic

Jamaican Chicken Sandwiches
burgers
corn on the cob
Layered Southwest Salad
potato salad
Stars and Strips Cupcakes
watermelon

utensils are always acceptable. This is the easiest situation to ask guests to bring some of the food, so even the busiest host can handle the food preparation. Barbecues are a great way to celebrate summer holidays (Fourth of July, Labor Day or Father's Day), a graduation or a birthday with the minimum impact on your busy schedule.

Holiday Dinners: When you host your family for a holiday dinner, don't get too far away from the traditional celebration. It's surprising how many people find tradition important,

especially at major holiday meals. And food is one of the things many people don't want to change. Instead, plan minor changes, such as replacing a side dish with something new, changing the turkey stuffing or adding another dessert.

These are definitely occasions when you can ask for help. Enlist family members to bring a dish (usually a side dish, rolls or a dessert). Or, invite one or two good cooks to help you in the kitchen. Also decide what can be done the day before or early in the day.

Christmas Cookie Baking Party: Baking cookies for the holidays is something many bakers enjoy and don't like to give up. However, with today's busy lifestyles, it's getting more difficult to find several days to devote to baking and decorating cookies. Ask a small group of fellow bakers (three or four for a small or medium kitchen or as many as five or six for a large kitchen with two ovens) to join you for a day in the kitchen. Each person brings their favorite recipe and the ingredients to make it or the already-prepared dough for two recipes, plus any necessary ingredients for finishing. Guests work together to roll out, shape or drop cookie dough, then bake and

the same container. It is also a good idea to serve a light lunch midway through the day.

Some friends have turned the cookie baking get-together into an annual event. Sometimes the best part is getting together ahead of time over afternoon tea or dinner at a restaurant to plan the day. Your goal is to get a variety of different kinds of cookies and have fun while you're doing it.

Cooking Party: Getting people together to cook can be a fun way to entertain. Keep the group small; noncooks tend to enjoy the insight into cooking and experienced cooks will enjoy trying something new. Things to try include making pasta, pizza or a gourmet dinner. As host you supply the ingredients, the recipes, the equipment and the kitchen. You'll be surprised how much your friends will enjoy getting covered in flour, learning to operate a pasta machine or showing off their knife skills.

Afternoon Tea: An mid-afternoon tea is an easy-to-plan get-together; food can be simple and the guest list short. Typically this is a gathering of women or little girls and their mothers. Food should be a mix of savory and sweet: finger sandwiches, a special cheese,

decorate the cookies. Finished cookies are divided up so everyone goes home with a great assortment of cookies.

Before planning a cookie bake, take a look at your kitchen with a critical eye. Decide how many people can comfortably work in the area and determine how the group can best use the space. Do you have enough baking sheets and tools or do you need your friends to bring baking equipment? Guests should bring plenty of storage containers to carry home cookies—it's best not to combine different cookies in

Making the Perfect Pot of Tea

Should you use loose tea leaves or tea bags? Loose tea can make a more elegant presentation. If this is your choice, make sure you have a tea pot with an infuser, or a tea ball small enough to fit into your tea pot but large enough to to hold the tea leaves (usually 1 teaspoon per each 5- or 6-ounce cup of tea). Tea bags are more convenient and they do give you the flexibility of serving everyone a different variety of tea.

You will also need a tea pot large enough to make at least one cup of tea per guest. Or, if the group is large or guests are divided between tea and herbal tea, use a second tea pot. The tea needs to be made at the last minute once your guests have arrived. First, warm the tea pot by adding hot tap water or water that has been brought to a boil. Then fill a kettle with cold water and bring it to a boil over high heat, being careful not to let it boil for longer than a minute. Meanwhile, empty the tea pot of the hot water. Add tea leaves to the infuser or tea ball and place it in the tea pot. You may also use tea bags (one bag per cup of tea). Pour the boiling water into the tea pot; let it stand (this is called steeping the tea) for 3 to 5 minutes (it's best to follow the steeping directions on the package), then remove the infuser. Serve immediately.

You may need to replenish the pot several times. If you choose to offer guests a selection of tea bags, then you may not want to prepare a pot of tea. Instead, bring a tea pot of boiling water to the table or have an electric kettle on a side table.

For herbal, green and white teas, be sure to follow the package directions, because they may vary from the above instructions.

scones, mini muffins, tea breads and dainty cookies are all good menu items. Tea made in a tea pot is a must, although lemonade can be substituted for girls who don't like tea. Frilly-looking china completes the perfect picture, but actually any tableware can be used.

If you plan to include your children at the tea, let them help with the

Poached Salmon with
Tarragon Cream Sauce

asparagus spears/carrot strips

Lemon Poppy Seed Muffins

Chunky Caramel
Nut Brownies
with
ice cream

This is your chance to add flowers and candles to the table. Don't forget the music; it will help set the mood. Plan an appetizer and serve it with wine or your favorite nonalcoholic beverage, especially if you and your partner need to wind down after a busy day. Then move on to a main course followed by dessert and coffee. You don't need to spend all day in the kitchen. Always remember that picking up some of the food from a gourmet shop or bakery is acceptable.

preparation. They can arrange a bunch of daisies, carnations or mums in a vase, set the table and make the lemonade. Together you can decide who will sit where.

Romantic Dinner for Two:

Valentine's Day is an ideal time for a party just for two. However, there's no need to wait for a special day—romance works any day. The food can be simple or fancy, but the important thing is that it be delicious and just what your partner loves. Even your regular weeknight meal can be made romantic, if your children are spending the evening with their friends and you make time for a leisurely meal.

Super Bowl Party: In recent
years it has become popular to host a Super Bowl party on that special game day. Plan a laid back get-together with simple but hearty food, like chilis, soups, sandwiches, casseroles, desserts and beverages. Remember that the game is the focus of the day, so food should be available throughout most of the game. A buffet presentation is ideal. Keep chilis and soups hot in a slow cooker and replenish sandwiches and salads periodically, especially just before half time.

Slow Cooker Cheese Dip
with tortilla chips
Lasagna Supreme
Shredded BBQ Chicken Sandwiches
coleslaw
tossed green salad
Italian or ranch dressing
Apple-Walnut Glazed Spiced Baby Cakes
Easy Mocha Brownies

Theme Parties: There are an infinite number of themes you can build a party around—from old standards like birthday parties, bridal or baby showers, or Halloween and New Year's Eve parties to unusual ideas such as parties to celebrate Summer Solstice, Mardi Gras, Chinese New Year or the Academy Awards. This is your opportunity to use your creativity and choose clever games and contests, appropriate food, creative decorations and fun activities to fit the party theme.

Hosts often think costumes are a good way to carry out a theme party. They are, but if your friends are busy people, this may be difficult for them to manage. Instead, suggest that they all dress in the same colors for your First Day of Winter Party (for example, blue and white), sport their favorite team's hat to celebrate the opening of baseball season, or ask your girlfriends to add a boa to their outfit when they come for tea. It's fun but a lot less work, and it allows anyone with the time and creativity to expand on your suggestion.

Bridal Shower

Creamy Citrus Fruit Dip

bruschetta with chopped tomatoes and capers

Chicken, Asparagus & Mushroom Bake

salad greens with grape tomatoes

balsamic vinaigrette

Zucchini Orange Bread with butter

Wedding Bells

Open House: An open house is a unique way to solve some entertaining dilemmas. If you want to host all your friends for the Christmas holidays but wonder how you'll ever find a time that will work for everyone, or you want to show off your brand new townhouse, but it will accommodate only a dozen people at one time, an open house may just be the solution you're looking for. Schedule the party from noon until 7:00. Guests can drop in at their convenience and they will feel comfortable even if they stay only for an hour.

Determining a menu can be as easy as serving an assortment of appetizers, soup, sandwiches, salad and cookies for dessert. Choose food that tastes great when it's hot and as it cools to room temperature or is tasty cold. For food safety, food should not sit out for more than two hours, so replenish everything as needed or every two hours, whichever comes first (see page 11 for more information).

You can also serve two different meals. For example, schedule the open house from 10:00 until 4:00 and serve brunch from 10:00 until 1:00, then switch to a luncheon menu. You can overlap menu items, if you wish. Serve biscuits filled with sliced ham for brunch, but change to ham and cheese sandwiches for lunch. Repeating the dessert between the two menus is also a good idea.

Spur-of-the-Moment Entertaining: Everyone envies the host that can provide a meal for guests on short notice. Actually, all it takes to accomplish this is advance planning—before you know guests are coming. Create a menu or two and keep the ingredients on hand to make the meal.

For example, plan a casserole or pasta dish. Pasta (or rice) can be stored for a long time. Keep cubed cooked chicken, ground beef or individually frozen chicken breasts or thin-cut pork chops in the freezer; you can thaw these quickly in the microwave oven while you're cooking the pasta. Combined with canned condensed soup, chopped onion, a frozen vegetable and cheese, you have the makings of a delicious casserole. For the best flavor, use the frozen meat and poultry every three months for a family dinner—just be sure to replace it. For a quick pasta dish, cook pasta and top it with a bottled pasta sauce simmered with 2 tablespoons of red wine. Or, you can cook any fresh

vegetables you find in the refrigerator in olive oil and toss them with cooked pasta and grated Parmesan cheese.

Complete the meal with a salad of fresh tomatoes or salad greens, if you have them. Keep several dessert choices, such as ice cream or an unbaked pie in the freezer. You can make a quick fruit crisp with fresh or canned fruit and a topping of flour, brown sugar, oats and butter. So the next time old friends drop by in the late afternoon, calmly invite them to join you for dinner. They will be praising your hosting skills to everyone.

Planning the Menu

For some of you this may be the most daunting of a host's responsibilities—creating the menu for your party. However, with the guidelines that follow you can learn what foods go together, how much to serve, how to control your budget, and how to manage it all if you have a busy life.

Where to start: If you've been following this party-planning guide, you should already have a reason or theme for your party, know who your guests will be, know what time of day the party will start, and have decided on an entertaining style (buffet, dinner party, picnic or tea). Now you can let the theme dictate the menu. If you've chosen an Irish theme, build your menu around Irish cuisine or give non-Irish dishes clever Gaelic names or serve an assortment of green food. For a barbecue, choose simple foods that you know everyone will like and add an appropriate dessert or two.

When planning menus you need to keep in mind how much space you have for the buffet, the size of your kitchen and what kind of equipment you have. You don't want to plan 15 dishes when the buffet table can only hold 10. Nor should you plan 4 baked dishes that need to come out of the oven 10 minutes before serving if your oven is small or 3 dishes that require different baking temperatures.

What's the budget: Most of us entertain on a budget, so determine how much you feel comfortable spending for your party. Remember, you may need to pay for invitations and decorations as well as food and beverages.

For a modest budget for a buffet meal, keep in mind bargain ingredients, such as pasta, rice, whole chicken, chicken drumsticks, ground beef, eggs and potatoes. Turn these ingredients into dishes like lasagna, chili, chicken casseroles, stews, quiches and soups. If you love your

---

Dinner party menu for six:

You decide to serve Stuffed Flank Steak (page 68). The flank steak in this recipe is marinated in a red wine, soy sauce and garlic mixture, drained, then filled with spinach, roasted red peppers and blue cheese. To accompany it you could serve Vegetable Couscous (page 213). You'll want to avoid side dishes that repeat flavors in the entrée, so a garlicky rice and spinach dish would not be the best choice. You'll also want to avoid strong flavors in the side dishes because the stuffed flank steak includes blue cheese and soy sauce.

Mashed potatoes or a seasoned long-grain and wild rice mixture would also complement the Stuffed Flank Steak. Steamed green beans, tossed with melted butter, would provide beautiful, bright color color and a tossed salad will contribute crispness.

that fruits and vegetables purchased in their peak season of availability are more likely to be reasonably priced. Spring and early summer is the best time for asparagus, broccoli, green onions and strawberries, so find a way to feature them in your menu. Summer fruits like berries, peaches, nectarines and melons are reasonably priced as are green beans, summer squash and tomatoes. And in the fall, apples, squash and pork are good menu choices.

What's the goal: When serving a meal to guests, you want to satisfy their hunger with food that looks good and tastes great. The goal to meal planning is to achieve balance among foods with contrasting colors, textures and flavors.

What goes with what: When planning a menu, select the entrée first (for a full-meal buffet, choose one entrée, then any additional entrées) and pair it with dishes that will complement it in

slow cooker, bring it out for your party. Less tender, less expensive cuts of meat are best suited for slow cooking and will help keep costs down. If you have more time than money, prepare most of the food yourself: buy lettuce and salad greens and tear them for the tossed salad rather than buying already washed, mixed and bagged greens; prepare your own dips and spreads; and make desserts from scratch. Look for sales at the grocery store or join a warehouse club that offers quality foods at great savings.

What's the season: Keep in mind

appearance, flavor and texture. Colors and shapes should work together to create a pleasing presentation. A meal containing three foods of a similar color is not visually interesting. Avoid pairing dishes that include similar size pieces—a stew or casserole with small chunks of meat and vegetables should not be paired with a chopped tomato and cucumber salad and western-style corn. It's just too many busy looking dishes.

Foods served together should offer some contrast in texture. Soft cheese spreads with crisp crackers, creamy dips with crunchy chips, and tender meats with crisp salads are examples of foods that complement each other.

Complementary flavors make meals interesting. Half the pleasure of eating a spicy burrito is knowing that cooling sour cream and a cold beer are close at hand. Balance spicy foods with ones that quench the fire. Combine bland foods with flavorful ones. Do not repeat strong flavors, such as garlic, blue cheese, or ginger in the same meal. Balance and moderation are important. Don't serve too many rich creamy dishes at the same meal, and don't get carried away with too much ethnic fusion. Finish a rich meal with a light, refreshing fresh fruit dessert. If you want to serve a rich and sinful dessert, choose a main course that is light.

Keep in mind any special dietary needs of your guests. For a dinner party, choose an appropriate menu for the vegetarian or the guest that has diabetes or is dieting. (Refer to the index in the back of the book for Low-Fat Recipes and Diabetic Recipes.) When creating a menu for a buffet, all foods don't need to meet the requirements of those on special diets, but make sure they have enough to eat and several choices so they can enjoy the meal. Guest with food allergies should, of course, always be accommodated.

Not enough time and not enough help: It can be difficult to entertain if you don't have a lot of time to devote to cooking for your party and don't have someone to help. If you have little cooking experience, it can be daunting to coordinate the preparation of many dishes so they will all be ready at the same time. (See "Knowing what you need to do" on page 27. Including some make-ahead dishes in your menu that can be quickly reheated just before the party can help. Include foods that can be served cold or at room temperature, ready-to-serve items from the deli or gourmet shop, or a dessert from the best bakery in town can help you manage your time more wisely.

Cooking the entrée in a slow cooker will also free up time in your preparation schedule.

Do a practice run: Preparing your menu for practice a week or so before your party will give you confidence that the menu items complement each other. It will also allow you to make note of minor adjustments you might want to make to recipes you've never prepared before: you might want to turn down the heat in a Tex-Mex recipe and up the salt in another. You can even review how the food will look on the serving dishes you're planning to use. And finally, it will give you an idea of how long it will take for you to prepare the food and decide where you need preparation shortcuts. Nothing instills confidence in an inexperienced host like a trial run.

Even if you're a seasoned cook, you shouldn't try new recipes when entertaining without a trial run. You may be confident enough in your cooking and entertaining skills to forego a practice run through of your entire menu, but be sure to try any new recipes ahead of time. It's also a good idea to taste the wine with the entrée you plan to serve to avoid any surprises at your dinner party.

Organizing the Details

Most kitchens aren't organized to make entertaining easy. Reorganizing prior to a large party that will require hours of preparation will help the work go more smoothly. Now is the time to take a critical look at your kitchen to determine if you need to free up some counter space, if you need to replenish pantry supplies, and if you have all the necessary equipment and serving pieces.

Making room to work: Do you really need all of those things on the counter? If your kitchen is like most, there's a pile of mail off to the side, small appliances you won't need when preparing for the party, a cookie jar and a stack of school books. Remove anything you won't actually need for party preparation.

Making the most of your pantry: First check to see that all herbs and spices you plan to use are fresh. If any are more than six

months old, replace them. Ingredients like flour, oil, butter, eggs, nuts, coffee, tea, soft drinks and beer have limited shelf life. Flour and oil should have mild fresh aromas. Flour shouldn't be kept longer than six months at room temperature and oil is best used within 3 months. Check the expiration dates on butter and eggs. Beer and some soft drinks have expiration dates as well; beer is best if used within a month or two of purchase. Tea and soft drinks can be stored up to six months. An open can of ground coffee is best used within a few weeks while coffee beans in an open package remain fresh for about one month. Nuts are high in fat; when they are stored at room temperature they can become rancid within a few weeks. You can keep them fresh up to four months by storing them in the refrigerator. Always taste nuts before you use them (even if you just purchased them), because rancid nuts will spoil any food they're used in.

Storage solutions: You'll need extra storage space for your party, especially in the refrigerator to store perishables and maybe in the freezer. If the fridge or freezer is due for a good cleaning, do it now. If your kitchen is small,

you may have to set up a card table in an adjoining room to hold nonperishables. You don't want to take valuable counter space for these items.

Knowing what you need to do

Before you actually dive into preparation, you need to make another plan. This time make a list of all that you need to do. It's the best way to ensure that you don't forget something important. Here are some suggestions for things that need to be done:

- Write down your menu.
- Tag the recipes you plan to use so they can be easily found. Or, better yet, photocopy them so you have

ready access to them.

- List all items you will need to purchase—from groceries and beverages to flowers, kitchen tools, paper goods and serving pieces.

- Reorganize the list into two or three lists. One list should be nonperishable groceries, tools, paper goods and serving pieces that can be purchased several weeks in advance; it will feel good to have some of the shopping out of the way. The second list should be items that can be purchased three or four days before the party. The third list is for last-minute things, such as picking up the cake from the bakery, the centerpiece from the florist and the raspberries from the produce market. Often list two and three can be combined.

- Make a list of noncooking tasks that need to be done, such as washing the wine glasses, setting the table or organizing the buffet table.

- Make a list of all the cooking and baking that needs to be done.

Timing is everything: Even experienced hosts need a game plan! And the bigger the event the more important the game plan becomes. Make a flow chart that lists everything you or someone else needs to do; it can be all tasks for the week before the party or just the day of the party. Some hosts prefer to put each item of the flow chart on a 3×5-inch note card, which leaves room to write notes.

Don't wait until the last minute: The beauty of planning weeks in advance for a big event is that you can spread out the work over several weeks. If an unforseen complication comes along the day before the party, you'll be delighted that many tasks are already accomplished. Unless your party is a spur-of-the-moment event, don't leave everything until the last minute. It's easy to misjudge how long tasks will take to complete or to anticipate all that can go wrong. If your entire day is dedicated to preparing for the party, it will be difficult to accommodate last-minute emergencies.

Get help: The bigger the event, the more likely you will need help. You might need help prior to or during the party; whether it's cooking, setting the table, decorating or collecting coats at the door, choose the the most dependable helper you can find.

Don't make yourself crazy: Entertaining can be stressful, especially if you have little experience. Plan realistically—a complicated menu, elaborate decorations or even too many last-minute dishes can set you up for problems. Evaluate your time and skill level and plan appropriately. No one expects you to be a master at entertaining on your first try. Guests will enjoy a good meal and pleasant conversation. As you're making lists and a flow chart, you can reevaluate what you've planned for yourself. There's still time to simplify the menu.

But what should you do if something goes wrong? If you forget to prepare one of the side dishes, no one needs to know. If the chicken entrée goes up in flames on the grill, have a back-up plan. Pull hamburger patties from freezer or send someone for a bucket of fried chicken. If you keep your cool, your guests will be impressed. Try to see the humor in any situation that comes up; it will make a great story to share for years to come.

Common Weights and Measures

Dash	=	less than ⅛ teaspoon
½ tablespoon	=	1½ teaspoons
1 tablespoon	=	3 teaspoons
2 tablespoons	=	⅛ cup
¼ cup	=	4 tablespoons
⅓ cup	=	5 tablespoons plus 1 teaspoon
½ cup	=	8 tablespoons
¾ cup	=	12 tablespoons
1 cup	=	16 tablespoons
½ pint	=	1 cup or 8 fluid ounces
1 pint	=	2 cups or 16 fluid ounces
1 quart	=	4 cups or 2 pints or 32 fluid ounces
1 gallon	=	16 cups or 4 quarts
1 pound	=	16 ounces

Decorating

A beautiful table with an eye-catching centerpiece puts the finishing touch on your dinner or buffet table and makes a delicious dinner just that much better. Decorations need not be expensive or elaborate. In fact, you can pick up a few things while you're at the supermarket that you can fashion into an attractive centerpiece.

Set the scene: You don't need to limit decorations to the table. You can start at the front door with a theme-appropriate wreath and in the entrance hall with a vase of flowers or an attractive decoration. This sets the mood, especially when the party has a theme. And it provides an instant conversation starter if your guests haven't met before.

Set the table: Take a little extra time to set a beautiful table for a dinner party with a tablecloth or placemats, napkins, tableware and glassware. A nice touch borrowed from a formal table setting (and a timesaver for you later) is to place the dessert silverware above the plate. You won't have to deal with it while you're serving dessert and coffee.

Decorate the table: Although a flower centerpiece may be the first thing you think of for decorating a dinner or buffet table, it doesn't have to be the only choice. If you'd rather spend your money on food than decorations, there are a lot of inexpensive ways to decorate. Candles keep for a long time and while some can be expensive, they can be reused many times. Place one single fat unscented candle in a shallow bowl surrounded by small colorful Christmas ornaments, unshelled nuts mixed with autumn leaves, seashells and polished pebbles. An arrangement of fruit in a bowl or on a shallow oblong plate is economical; you can pack the fruit in the kids' lunch boxes over the next few days. Flowering houseplants are always an option; the initial cost may be more, but you'll enjoy them for a

long time. Or, the plants can be your gift to the guest of honor.

Invest in a clear glass vase, bowl or tall container. Or, make a grouping of three simple containers of different heights. (Arrangements of an odd number of things often look better than a pair of containers.) Fill them with lemons and limes, or polished stones that support one beautiful orchid or lily. Let your imagination be your guide and keep it simple for greater impact.

Garnishing the food: Making the food look attractive is as important as making the table beautiful. Garnishing adds the finishing touch to dishes. When you're entertaining, time is limited so choose simple garnishes. Use one of the flavors in the dish or something that complements the dish in color and flavor. For example, if you use fresh herbs in a recipe, hold back a few sprigs for a simple garnish. Lemon and lime wedges or slices, lemon peel strips, tomato wedges, cherry tomatoes (in red or yellow), green onion tops, carrot curls and pepperoncini all are quick, easy ways to garnish savory dishes. For desserts, choose strawberries, raspberries, lemon slices, lime peel strips, or chocolate curls to add the perfect finishing touch. Not every dish needs a garnish; many are colorful enough alone. If the serving dish has a bold design, the food may not need a garnish. A few well placed touches go a long way.

Hosting the Party

Your job as host is to welcome guests, see that their coats are taken, get them a drink, direct them to the appetizers and introduce them to those they don't know. For a small group, these tasks are best done by two hosts. You can take turns, which will allow the cook to duck into the kitchen for final preparations. If you are the only host, that's a lot to do—plus you have to take care of the food as well. When the party is large, you may not always be able to greet guests at the door. But it's important to greet them as soon as possible.

Relax: When you are planning your schedule for the day of the party, make time for a break. It should be long enough to allow you to get dressed and catch your breath. Then you can return to the kitchen and any last-minute details.

You're the cook *and* the only host: This can be tricky especially when there are a lot of guests. Either plan a menu that requires little last-minute touches or designate a helper. The helper can get the prepared food to the buffet. A close friend or family member can serve as an assistant host. The two of you can share the hosting duties as guests arrive and free you for a quick trip to the kitchen.

Don't let a guest hide: As the host, make sure that every guest has found someone to talk with. Draw shy people into a group who share similar interests. Encourage guests to circulate. If a small group stays together for a long period of time, gracefully take one or two away and introduce them to another group. Or, ask them to help you in the kitchen for a few minutes.

What if conversation stalls: This is not often a problem with a large group but may be at a dinner party. If getting a conversation going is not your strong suit, be ready with a couple of funny or interesting stories that will help get conversation going again. Or, you can begin a discussion about a newsworthy current event. It's probably best to stay away from

Gifts for the Host

Many guests are kind enough to bring a gift for the host. It can be a bottle of wine, candy or flowers. Do not feel compelled to serve gifts of wine or food items at your event. Just be sure to tell the guest how much you will enjoy this gift another day. Flowers should be arranged in a vase and placed where they can be seen. They need not be added to the buffet or the dinner table.

politics and religion, but that doesn't mean the topic has to be innocuous. You know your friends and whether they can discuss a controversial topic without getting into a heated discussion.

Encourage guests to talk about themselves, a recent addition to their family, an upcoming trip or their new home. A great host learns to adroitly change the subject if someone goes on and on about something. If you don't think you can do this, let a close friend know before the party that you may need their help to redirect stalled conversations.

Special touches

Guests always appreciate any special touches that a host adds when entertaining. A blackboard menu is a fun way to let guests know what's on the menu. Propped up on the buffet table or hanging near where you serve appetizers or drinks, this can be another easy conversation starter. For an informal dinner party in which the guests don't all know each other, hand-lettered place cards are a great way to help people remember new names and it lets you decide where guests will sit. You can pair people with similar interests to encourage conversation. Try not to seat long-time friends together as they may focus on each other and not nearby guests. It's also a subtle way to pair a couple who you think might be great together—just sit back and see if the sparks fly!

Giving small brightly wrapped gifts to guests is a charming custom that your friends will talk about for a long time. Placing the gifts at each place setting with large gift tags with the recipients' names turns them into artful place cards.

Glossary

al dente: The literal translation of this Italian phrase is "to the tooth." It indicates a degree of doneness when cooking pasta. Al dente pasta is slightly firm and chewy, rather than soft.

Baste: Basting is the technique of brushing, spooning or pouring liquids over food, usually meat and poultry, as it cooks. It helps preserve moistness, adds flavor and gives foods an attractive appearance. Melted butter, pan drippings, broth or a combination of these ingredients are frequently used. Sometimes seasonings or flavorings are added.

Beat: Beating is the technique of stirring or mixing vigorously. Beating introduces air into egg whites, egg yolks and whipping cream; mixes two or more ingredients to form a homogeneous mixture; or makes a mixture smoother, lighter and creamier. Beating can be done with a variety of tools including a spoon, fork, wire whisk, rotary egg beater or electric mixer.

Blanch: Blanching means cooking foods, most often vegetables, briefly in boiling water and then quickly cooling them in cold water. Food is blanched for one or more of the following reasons: to loosen and remove skin (tomatoes, peaches, almonds); to enhance color and reduce bitterness (raw vegetables for crudités); and to extend storage life (raw vegetables to be frozen).

Blend: Blending is the technique of mixing together two or more ingredients until they are thoroughly combined. The ingredients may be blended together with an electric mixer or electric blender, or by hand, using a wooden spoon or wire whisk.

Boil: To bring to a boil means to heat a liquid until bubbles break the surface. Boiling refers to cooking food in boiling water. For a "full rolling boil," bubbles continue vigorously to break the surface and cannot be stirred away.

Braise: Braising is a moist-heat cooking method used to tenderize tough cuts of meat or fibrous vegetables. Food is first browned in fat and then gently simmered in a small amount of liquid in a tightly covered skillet until tender. This can be done on the rangetop or in the oven. The liquid, such as water, stock, wine or beer, often has finely chopped vegetables and herbs added for flavor.

Broil: Broiling is the technique of cooking foods a measured distance from a direct source of heat. Both gas and electric ovens provide a means of broiling. Some rangetops have built-in grills that provide another broiling option. Grilling on a barbecue grill also fits this broad definition of broiling. The goal of broiling is to brown the exterior without overcooking the interior. Generally, the thinner the food item the closer it should be to the heat source.

Brush: Brushing refers to the technique of applying liquid, such as melted butter, barbecue sauce or glaze, to the surface of food prior to or during cooking with a brush. It serves the same purpose as basting, preserving moistness, adding flavor and giving foods an attractive appearance.

Caramelize: Caramelizing is the technique of cooking sugar, sometimes with a small amount of water, to a very high temperature (between 310°F and 360°F) so that it melts into a clear brown liquid and develops a characteristic flavor. The color can vary from light golden brown to dark brown. Caramelized sugar, sometimes called "burnt sugar" is used in a variety of desserts and sauces.

Chill: Chilling is the technique of cooling foods, usually in the refrigerator or over ice, to a temperature of 35° to 40°F. A recipe or dish may require several hours or as long as overnight to chill thoroughly. To chill a large portion of a hot mixture, such as soup or chili, separate the mixture into several small containers for quicker cooling. To chill small amounts of hot food, place the food in a bowl or saucepan over a container of crushed ice or iced water. Or chill the food in the freezer for 20 to 30 minutes. Once chilled, a dish may be transported in a cooler or insulated case, preferably packed with ice packs.

Chop: Chopping is the technique of cutting food into small, irregularly shaped pieces. Although the term does not designate a specific size, most cooks would suggest that food be chopped into approximately ¼-inch pieces. Chopped food is larger than minced food and more irregularly cut than diced food. Recipe directions may call for a coarsely chopped or a finely chopped ingredient.

Coat: To coat means to cover food with an outer layer, usually fine or powdery, using ingredients such as flour, crumbs, cornmeal or sugar. With foods such as chicken, fish fillets and eggplant, this coating is preliminary to frying or baking and provides a crispy exterior. Such foods are often first rolled in eggs or milk so the coating adheres. Some cookies are coated with sugar before or after baking.

Combine: To combine is to mix two or more liquid or dry ingredients together to make them a uniform mixture.

Core: Coring means to remove the center seed-bearing structure of a fruit or vegetable. The most commonly cored foods are apples, pears, pineapple, zucchini and cucumbers. Coring can be accomplished with a small knife by first cutting the food into quarters and then cutting out the center core. A utensil specially designed to remove the core of specific whole fruits and vegetables is known as a corer. The most common corers are for apples, pears and pineapple.

Crumble: To crumble means to break food into small pieces of irregular size. It is usually done with the fingers. Ingredients often crumbled are blue cheese and bacon. Both foods can be purchased in the supermarket already crumbled.

Crush: Crushing means reducing a food, such as crackers, to small fine particles by rolling with a rolling pin or pounding with a mortar and pestle. A food processor or blender also works well. Fruit can be crushed to extract its juices. Garlic is sometimes crushed with the flat side of a knife blade or garlic press to release its flavor.

Cutting In: Cutting in is the technique used to combine a chilled solid fat such as shortening or butter with dry ingredients, such as flour, so that the resulting mixture is in coarse, small pieces. A fork, two table knives, fingers or a pastry blender may be used. If using a food processor, be careful not to overmix the ingredients. This process is used to make biscuits, scones, pie pastry and some cookies.

Deglaze: Deglazing is the technique used to retrieve the flavorful bits that adhere to a pan after a food, usually meat, has been browned and the excess fat has been drained. While the pan is still hot, a small amount of liquid (water, wine or broth) is added and stirred to loosen the browned bits in the pan. The resulting liquid is used as a base for sauces and gravies.

Degrease: Degreasing is a technique used to remove fat from the surface of a liquid, such as soup or stock. It can be accomplished in several ways. First remove the soup or stock from the heat and allow it to stand briefly until the fat rises. The quickest degreasing method is to skim off the fat using a large spoon. If the fat to be removed is animal fat, the liquid may be chilled; the animal fat will harden, making it easy to lift off.

Dice: To dice is to cut food into small cubes that are uniform in size, typically between ¼ and ½ of an inch. Dicing is distinguished from chopping and mincing by the care taken to achieve a uniform size for an attractive presentation.

Dot: This term, generally used in cooking as "to dot with butter," refers to cutting butter (or margarine) into small bits and scattering them over a food. This technique allows the butter to melt evenly. It also keeps the food moist, adds richness and can promote browning.

Dust: Dusting is a technique used to lightly coat a food, before or after cooking, with a powdery ingredient, such as flour or powdered sugar. The ingredient may be sprinkled on using your fingers or shaken from a small sieve or a container with holes on the top. A greased baking pan can be dusted with flour before it is filled, a technique also known as flouring.

Flake: To flake refers to the technique of separating or breaking off small pieces or layers of a food using a utensil, such as a fork.

For example, cooked fish fillets may be flaked for use in a salad or main dish.

Flour: To flour means to apply a light coating of flour to a food or piece of equipment. Applied to food, the flour dries the surface. This helps food brown better when frying or sautéing or keeps food, such as raisins, from sticking together. Baking pans are floured for better release characteristics and to produce thin, crisp crusts. Rolling pins, biscuit cutters, cookie cutters and work surfaces are floured to prevent doughs from sticking to them.

Fold: Folding is a specialized technique for combining two ingredients or mixtures, one of which usually has been aerated, such as whipped cream or egg whites. It is best done by placing the airy mixture on top of the other and with a rubber spatula, gently but quickly cutting through to the bottom and turning the ingredients over with a rolling motion. The bowl is rotated a quarter turn each time and the process repeated until the mixtures are combined, with as little loss in volume as possible. Care must be taken not to stir, beat or overmix. Fruit pieces, chips or nuts may be folded into an airy mixture using the same technique.

Fry: Frying refers to the technique of cooking foods in hot fat, usually vegetable oil. Proper fat temperature is critical to a successful result. The ideal temperature produces a crisp exterior and a moist, perfectly cooked interior. Too high a temperature will burn the food. Too low a temperature will result in food absorbing excessive fat. A deep-fat thermometer is essential to determining the temperature of the fat. Deep-fried foods are submerged or floated in hot fat in a large heavy saucepan or Dutch oven. Electric deep fryers fitted with wire baskets are available. Panfrying refers to cooking food in a skillet in a small amount of fat that does not cover the food.

Grate: Grating refers to the technique of making very small particles from a firm food like carrots, lemon peel or Parmesan cheese by rubbing it along a coarse surface with small, sharp protrusions, usually a kitchen grater or microplane. Food may also be grated in a food processor using the metal blade.

Knead: Kneading refers to the technique of manipulating bread dough in order to develop the protein in flour, called gluten, to ensure the structure of the finished product. Kneading also aids in combining the dough ingredients. Biscuit dough is lightly kneaded only about ten times whereas yeast doughs may be vigorously kneaded for several minutes.

Mash: To mash is to crush a food into a soft, smooth mixture, as in mashed potatoes or bananas. It can be done with a tool called a potato masher or with an electric mixer. Small amounts of food, such as one or two bananas or a few hard-cooked egg yolks, can be mashed with a fork. For best results, make sure that potatoes are fully cooked so they are soft enough to become completely smooth.

Mince: Mincing refers to the technique of chopping food into very tiny, irregular pieces. Minced food is smaller than chopped food. Flavorful seasonings, such as garlic and fresh herbs, are often minced to distribute their flavor more evenly throughout a dish.

Purée: To purée means to mash or strain a soft or cooked food until it has a smooth consistency. This can be done with a food processor, sieve, blender or food mill. For best results, the food must be naturally soft, such as raspberries or ripe pears, or cooked until it is completely tender. Puréed foods are used as sauces and as ingredients in other sweet or savory dishes. The term also refers to the foods that result from the process.

Reduce: To reduce is to boil a liquid, usually a sauce, until its volume has been decreased through evaporation. This results in a more intense flavor and thicker consistency. Typically sauces are reduced by one third or one half of their original volume. Use a pan with a wide bottom to shorten preparation time. The reduced product is referred to as a reduction. Since the flavor of the seasonings will also become concentrated when a sauce is reduced, add the seasonings to the sauce after it has been reduced.

Roast: Roasting involves cooking poultry and large tender cuts of meat in the oven in an uncovered pan. Roasting produces a nicely browned exterior and a moist interior. Roasting vegetables intensifies their natural sweetness. Vegetables, such as onions and carrots, can be roasted alongside meat. Many vegetables can be roasted and served as a side dish or used as ingredients in other dishes.

Roll Out: To roll out means to flatten dough into an even layer using a rolling pin. To roll out pastry or cookie dough, place the dough, which should be in the shape of a disc, on a floured surface, such as a counter, pastry cloth or a large cutting board. Lightly flour your hands and the rolling pin. Place the rolling pin across the center of the dough. With several light strokes, roll the rolling pin away from you toward the edge of the dough. Turn the dough a quarter turn and roll again from the center to the edge. Repeat this process until the dough is the desired thickness. If the dough becomes sticky, dust it and the rolling pin with flour. If the dough sticks to the surface, gently fold back the edge of the dough and dust the surface underneath the dough with flour.

Sauté: Sautéing is the technique of rapidly cooking or browning food in a small amount of fat in a skillet or sauté pan. The food is constantly stirred, turned or tossed to keep it from sticking or burning. Thin, tender cuts of meat, such as steaks, lamb chops, sliced pork tenderloin, flattened chicken breasts and fish fillets are candidates for sautéing. The objective is to brown the food on the outside in the time needed to cook the interior. This requires medium-high heat. Oil can withstand the higher heat needed for sautéing. For flavor, a little butter can be added to the oil, but do not use only butter or margarine, because it will burn before the food browns.

Sift: Sifting is the technique of passing a dry ingredient, such as flour or powdered sugar, through the fine mesh of a sieve or sifter for the purpose of breaking up lumps and making it lighter in texture. Sifting results in finer baked goods and smoother frostings. Most all-purpose flour is presifted, eliminating the need for sifting. Cake flour is generally sifted before using. Spoon the ingredient into the sieve and push it through the mesh screen using a metal spoon or rubber spatula.

Simmer: To simmer is to cook a liquid or a food in a liquid with gentle heat just below the boiling point. Simmering is indicated by small bubbles slowly rising to the surface of the liquid.

Sliver: To sliver is the technique of cutting food into thin strips or pieces. Basil and garlic are two ingredients that may be identified as slivered in a recipe. The word sliver may also refer to a long, thin strip of food or a small wedge of a pie.

Steam: Steaming is a method of cooking food, usually vegetables, in the steam given off by boiling water. The food is held above, but not in, the boiling or simmering water in a covered pan. The steam swirls around the food and cooks it with an intense, moist heat. Steaming helps to retain flavor, color, shape, texture and many of the vitamins and minerals. Steaming requires a two-pan steamer, a steamer basket or a bamboo steamer.

Toast: Toasting is the technique of browning foods by means of dry heat. Bread products, nuts, seeds and coconut are commonly toasted. Toasting is done in a toaster, toaster oven, oven, skillet or under the broiler. The purpose of toasting bread is to brown, crisp and dry it. Nuts, seeds and coconut are toasted to intensify their flavor.

Whip: To whip refers to the technique of beating ingredients, such as egg whites and whipping cream, with a wire whisk or electric mixer in order to incorporate air and increase their volume. This results in a light, fluffy texture.

Whisk: Whisking is the technique of stirring, beating or whipping foods with a wire whisk. If you do not have a whisk, you can use a wooden spoon if the purpose is to blend ingredients. For whipping foods, an electric mixer can be used instead.

Cook's Substitutions

If you don't have:	Use:
1 teaspoon baking powder	¼ teaspoon baking soda plus ⅝ teaspoon cream of tartar
½ cup firmly packed brown sugar	½ cup sugar mixed with 2 tablespoons molasses
1 ounce (1 square) unsweetened baking chocolate	3 tablespoons unsweetened cocoa plus 1 tablespoon shortening
3 ounces (3 squares) semisweet baking chocolate	3 ounces (½ cup) semisweet chocolate morsels
1 cup sweetened whipped cream	4½ ounces thawed frozen whipped topping
1 cup heavy cream (for baking, not whipping)	¾ cup whole milk plus ¼ cup butter
1 cup honey	1¼ cups granulated sugar plus ¼ cup water
1 package active dry yeast	1 cake compressed yeast
1 cup buttermilk	1 tablespoon lemon juice or vinegar plus milk to equal 1 cup (stir; let stand 5 minutes)
1 tablespoon cornstarch	2 tablespoons all-purpose flour or 2 teaspoons arrowroot
1 whole egg	2 egg yolks plus 1 teaspoon cold water
1 teaspoon vinegar	2 teaspoons lemon juice
1 cup whole milk	1 cup skim milk plus 2 tablespoons melted butter
1 cup sour cream	1 cup plain yogurt

Appetizers & Beverages

Rosemary-Scented Nut Mix

2 tablespoons unsalted butter
2 cups pecan halves
1 cup unsalted macadamia nuts
1 cup walnuts
1 teaspoon dried rosemary, crushed
½ teaspoon salt
¼ teaspoon red pepper flakes

1. Preheat oven to 300°F. Melt butter in large saucepan over low heat. Add pecans, macadamia nuts and walnuts; mix well. Add rosemary, salt and red pepper flakes; cook and stir about 1 minute.

2. Pour mixture onto ungreased nonstick baking sheet. Bake 15 minutes, stirring mixture occasionally.   *Makes 16 servings*

Alouette® 7-Layer "Fiesta" Dip

1 cup chopped tomatoes
1 cup chopped bell peppers
1 cup canned corn, drained
1 cup sliced scallions
1 (6.5-ounce) package ALOUETTE® Cilantro Lime or Garlic & Herbs
    Spreadable Cheese
1 cup shredded lettuce
½ cup sliced black olives

In a 1-quart clear glass bowl, layer ingredients in order beginning with tomatoes and ending with olives. Cover and chill for 1 hour for flavors to blend.

Serve with your favorite tortilla chips.   *Makes 6 servings*

Rosemary-Scented Nut Mix

Festive Franks

1 can (8 ounces) reduced-fat crescent roll dough
5½ teaspoons barbecue sauce
⅓ cup finely shredded reduced-fat sharp Cheddar cheese
8 hot dogs
¼ teaspoon poppy seeds (optional)
Additional barbecue sauce (optional)

1. Preheat oven to 350°F. Spray large baking sheet with nonstick cooking spray; set aside.

2. Unroll dough and separate into 8 triangles. Cut each triangle in half lengthwise to make 2 triangles. Lightly spread barbecue sauce over each triangle. Sprinkle with cheese.

3. Cut each hot dog in half; trim off rounded ends. Place one hot dog piece at large end of one dough triangle. Roll up jelly-roll style from wide end. Place point-side down on prepared baking sheet. Sprinkle with poppy seeds, if desired. Repeat with remaining hot dog pieces and dough.

4. Bake 13 minutes or until dough is golden brown. Cool 1 to 2 minutes on baking sheet. Serve with additional barbecue sauce for dipping, if desired.

Makes 16 servings

BelGioioso® Gorgonzola Spread

2 cups BELGIOIOSO® Mascarpone
½ cup BELGIOIOSO® Gorgonzola
2 tablespoons chopped fresh basil
½ cup chopped walnuts
Sliced apples and pears

In small bowl, combine BelGioioso Mascarpone, BelGioioso Gorgonzola and basil. Mix to blend well. Transfer mixture to serving bowl; cover and refrigerate 2 hours. Before serving, sprinkle with walnuts and arrange sliced apples and pears around bowl.

Makes 8 servings

Tip: This spread can also be served with fresh vegetables, crackers, Melba toast or bread.

Festive Franks

Piña Colada Punch

5 cups DOLE® Pineapple Juice, divided
1 can (15 ounces) real cream of coconut
1 liter lemon-lime soda
2 limes
1½ cups light rum (optional)
    Ice cubes
    Mint sprigs

● Chill all ingredients.

● Blend 2 cups pineapple juice with cream of coconut in blender. Combine puréed mixture with remaining 3 cups pineapple juice, soda, juice of 1 lime, rum, if desired, and ice. Garnish with 1 sliced lime and mint.
Makes 15 servings

Hot Spinach Dip

1 (15-ounce) container ricotta cheese
1 cup sour cream
1 (10-ounce) package frozen chopped spinach, thawed and
    squeezed dry
2 (5-ounce) cans HORMEL® chunk ham, drained and flaked
¾ cup (3 ounces) grated fresh Parmesan cheese
2 green onions, thinly sliced
1 (16-ounce) round loaf bread, unsliced

In food processor, blender or electric mixer, combine ricotta cheese and sour cream; process until smooth. Stir in spinach, chunk ham, Parmesan cheese and green onions. Cut 1-inch slice off top of bread; reserve. Remove bread from inside of loaf, retaining ¾-inch shell; cut bread from inside of loaf into bite-size cubes. Pour cheese mixture into bread shell; replace top, wrap in foil and place on large baking sheet. Bake at 350°F 1 to 1½ hours or until heated through. Arrange heated loaf and bread cubes on large serving platter.
Makes 6 cups or 24 servings

Piña Colada Punch

Mini Taco Quiches

1 pound lean ground beef
⅓ cup chopped onions
1 can (8 ounces) tomato sauce
⅓ cup sliced black olives
1 package (1¼ ounces) taco seasoning mix
2 tablespoons *Frank's*® *RedHot*® Original Cayenne Pepper Sauce
1 egg, beaten
4 flour tortillas (10 inches)
⅓ cup sour cream
½ cup (2 ounces) shredded Cheddar cheese

1. Preheat oven to 350°F. Grease 12 muffin pan cups. Set aside.

2. Cook beef and onions in large nonstick skillet until meat is browned; drain. Remove from heat. Stir in tomato sauce, olives, ¼ cup water, taco seasoning, **Frank's RedHot** Sauce and egg; mix well.

3. Using 4-inch cookie cutter, cut each flour tortilla into 3 rounds. Fit each tortilla round into prepared muffin cup. Fill each tortilla cup with ¼ cup meat mixture. Top each with sour cream and cheese.

4. Bake 25 minutes or until heated through.   *Makes 12 servings*

Prep Time: 20 minutes
Cook Time: 30 minutes

Brandy Ham Spread

1 cup (6 ounces) chopped CURE 81® ham
¾ cup mayonnaise or salad dressing
1 tablespoon brandy
1 tablespoon sweet pickle relish
Assorted crackers

Position knife blade in food processor bowl; add ham. Process until ham is coarsely ground. In bowl, combine mayonnaise, ham, brandy and pickle relish. Cover and refrigerate 1 hour. Serve with crackers.   *Makes 1½ cups or 8 servings*

Mini Taco Quiches

Slow Cooker Cheese Dip

1 pound ground beef
1 pound Italian sausage
1 package (1 pound) processed cheese, cubed
1 can (11 ounces) sliced jalapeño peppers, drained
1 medium onion, diced
½ pound Cheddar cheese, cubed
1 package (8 ounces) cream cheese, cubed
1 container (8 ounces) cottage cheese
1 container (8 ounces) sour cream
1 can (8 ounces) diced tomatoes, drained
3 cloves garlic, minced
Salt and pepper

Slow Cooker Directions

1. Cook and stir ground beef and sausage in medium skillet over medium-high heat; drain. Transfer to slow cooker.

2. Add processed cheese, jalapeño peppers, onion, Cheddar cheese, cream cheese, cottage cheese, sour cream, tomatoes and garlic to slow cooker. Season with salt and pepper.

3. Cover; cook on HIGH 1½ to 2 hours or until cheeses are melted. Serve with crackers or tortilla chips.   *Makes 16 to 18 servings*

Creamy Citrus Fruit Dip

¼ cup low-fat vanilla yogurt
2 teaspoons lemon juice
1 packet sugar substitute
¼ teaspoon vanilla
1 cup honeydew or cantaloupe cubes

In a small bowl, combine all ingredients, except melon. Stir until well blended. Serve with melon.   *Makes 2 servings*

Slow Cooker Cheese Dip

East Meets West Cocktail Franks

1 cup prepared sweet and sour sauce
1½ tablespoons rice vinegar or cider vinegar
1 tablespoon grated fresh ginger _or_ 1 teaspoon dried ginger
1 tablespoon dark sesame oil
½ teaspoon chile oil (optional)
1 package (12 ounces) HEBREW NATIONAL® Cocktail Beef Franks
2 tablespoons chopped cilantro or chives

Combine sweet and sour sauce, vinegar, ginger, sesame oil and chile oil in medium saucepan. Bring to a boil over medium heat. Cook 5 minutes or until thickened. Add cocktail franks; cover and cook until heated through. Transfer to chafing dish; sprinkle with cilantro. Serve with frilled wooden picks.

Makes 12 appetizer servings (2 cocktail franks per serving)

Mini-Marinated Beef Skewers

1 boneless beef top sirloin steak (about 1 pound)
2 tablespoons soy sauce
2 tablespoons dry sherry
1 tablespoon dark sesame oil
2 cloves garlic, minced
18 cherry tomatoes
Lettuce leaves (optional)

1. Cut beef crosswise into ⅛-inch slices. Place in large plastic bag. Combine soy sauce, sherry, sesame oil and garlic in cup; pour over steak. Seal bag; turn to coat. Marinate in refrigerator at least 30 minutes or up to 2 hours.

2. Soak 18 (6-inch) wooden skewers 20 minutes in water to cover.

3. Drain steak; discard marinade. Weave beef accordion-fashion onto skewers. Place on rack of broiler pan.

4. Broil 4 to 5 inches from heat 4 minutes. Turn skewers over; broil 4 minutes or until beef is barely pink in center.

5. Garnish each skewer with one cherry tomato; place on lettuce-lined platter. Serve warm or at room temperature.

Makes 9 servings

East Meets West Cocktail Franks

Peppered Shrimp Skewers

⅓ **cup teriyaki sauce**
⅓ **cup ketchup**
 2 **tablespoons dry sherry or water**
 2 **tablespoons peanut butter**
 1 **teaspoon hot pepper sauce**
¼ **teaspoon ground ginger**
32 **raw large shrimp (about 1½ pounds)**
 2 **large yellow bell peppers**
32 **fresh sugar snap peas, trimmed**

1. To prevent burning, soak 16 (12-inch) wooden skewers in water at least 20 minutes before assembling kabobs.

2. Coat rack of broiler pan with nonstick cooking spray; set aside.

3. Combine teriyaki sauce, ketchup, sherry, peanut butter, pepper sauce and ginger in small saucepan. Bring to a boil, stirring constantly. Reduce heat to low; simmer, uncovered, 1 minute. Remove from heat; set aside.

4. Peel and devein shrimp, leaving tails intact.

5. Cut each bell pepper lengthwise into 4 quarters; remove stems and seeds. Cut each quarter crosswise into 4 equal pieces. Thread 2 shrimp, bell pepper pieces and 2 sugar snap peas onto each skewer; place on prepared broiler pan. Brush with teriyaki sauce mixture.

6. Broil 4 inches from heat 3 minutes; turn. Brush with teriyaki sauce mixture; broil 2 minutes longer or until shrimp turn pink. Discard any remaining teriyaki sauce mixture. Transfer skewers to serving plate. Garnish, if desired.

Makes 16 servings

Peppered Shrimp Skewer

Golden Artichoke Dip

1 envelope LIPTON® RECIPE SECRETS® Golden Onion Soup Mix*
1 can (14 ounces) artichoke hearts, drained and chopped
1 cup HELLMANN'S® or BEST FOODS® Real Mayonnaise
1 container (8 ounces) sour cream
1 cup shredded Swiss or mozzarella cheese (about 4 ounces)

*Also terrific with LIPTON® RECIPE SECRETS® Savory Herb with Garlic or Onion Soup Mix.

1. Preheat oven to 350°F. In 1-quart casserole, combine all ingredients.

2. Bake uncovered 30 minutes or until heated through.

3. Serve with your favorite dippers. *Makes 3 cups dip or 12 servings*

Variation: For a cold artichoke dip, omit Swiss cheese. Stir in, if desired, ¼ cup grated Parmesan cheese. Do not bake.

Tip: For a quick party fix or anytime treat, try these CLASSIC LIPTON DIPS: Combine 1 envelope Lipton Recipe Secrets Onion, Ranch, Savory Herb with Garlic, Onion Mushroom, Beefy Onion, Beefy Mushroom or Vegetable Soup Mix with 1 container (16 ounces) sour cream. Chill and serve with your favorite dippers.

Cranberry-Lime Party Punch

7½ cups low-calorie cranberry juice cocktail
½ cup fresh lime juice
6 packets sugar substitute *or* equivalent of ¼ cup sugar
2 cups ice cubes
1 cup sugar-free ginger ale or sugar-free lemon-lime soda
1 lime, sliced
Fresh cranberries for garnish (optional)

1. Combine cranberry juice, lime juice and sugar substitute in punch bowl; stir until sugar substitute dissolves.

2. Stir in ice, ginger ale and lime slices; garnish with fresh cranberries, if desired.
Makes 10 (8-ounce) servings

Golden Artichoke Dip

Hot Mulled Cider

1 orange
1 lemon
12 whole cloves
6 cups apple cider
⅓ cup sugar
3 cinnamon sticks
12 whole allspice berries

1. Poke 6 evenly spaced holes around orange and lemon with point of wooden skewer. Insert whole cloves into holes. Cut slice out of orange to include all cloves. Cut remainder of orange into thin slices. Repeat procedure with lemon.

2. Combine all ingredients in medium saucepan. Bring just to a simmer over medium heat. *Do not boil.* Reduce heat to low; cook 5 minutes. Pour cider through strainer into mugs. Discard fruit and seasonings. Garnish as desired.

Makes 6 cups or 8 servings

Pesto Filled Brie

1 (13.2- or 17.6-ounce) wheel ALOUETTE® Baby Brie®
1 small clove garlic
1 bunch fresh basil *or* 1½ teaspoons dried basil leaves
Freshly squeezed juice of 1 lemon
4 tablespoons unsalted butter, softened, divided
⅛ teaspoon freshly ground black pepper
1 tablespoon chopped pine nuts or walnuts
1 tablespoon chopped fresh parsley *or* 1½ teaspoons dried parsley flakes

Split Alouette Baby Brie horizontally into two layers. Set aside. In food processor or blender, chop garlic. Add enough fresh basil leaves to make about ½ cup. Add lemon juice, 2 tablespoons butter and pepper; process until smooth. Stir in nuts. Spread filling evenly onto cut side of one layer of cheese and top with second layer, cut side down. Spread remaining 2 tablespoons butter around edge of cheese. Sprinkle with parsley. To serve, cut into wedges.   *Makes 8 to 12 servings*

Hint: For best results, prepare 24 hours prior to serving to allow flavors to blend.

Hot Mulled Cider

Beefy Pinwheels

1 package (8 ounces) cream cheese
¼ cup chopped pimiento-stuffed green olives
2 tablespoons prepared horseradish mustard
6 (6- to 7-inch) flour tortillas
12 small slices deli roast beef
6 green onions, tops included

1. Place unwrapped cream cheese in small microwavable bowl. Microwave at HIGH 15 seconds or until softened.

2. Add olives and mustard, mix well.

3. Spread about 2 tablespoons cream cheese mixture over each tortilla. Top each with 2 overlapping slices of beef.

4. Place onion on one edge of tortilla, trimming onion to fit diameter of tortilla. Roll up tortilla jelly-roll fashion. Cut each roll into slices to serve.

Makes 6 beef rolls or 8 to 10 servings

Prep Time: 15 minutes

Pepper and Parsley Logs

1 packet (1 ounce) HIDDEN VALLEY® The Original Ranch® Salad
Dressing & Seasoning Mix
8 ounces cream cheese, softened
2 teaspoons cracked black pepper
2 teaspoons chopped fresh parsley

Combine dressing mix and cream cheese. Divide in half; chill until firm. Roll into two 1½-inch logs, coating one with pepper and the other with parsley. Wrap in plastic wrap; chill.

Makes 2 logs

Serving Suggestion: Spread on crackers or bread.

Beefy Pinwheels

Caponata

**1 medium eggplant (about 1 pound), peeled and cut into ½-inch
  pieces**
1 can (14½ ounces) diced Italian plum tomatoes, undrained
1 medium onion, chopped
1 red bell pepper, cut into ½-inch pieces
½ cup medium-hot salsa
¼ cup extra-virgin olive oil
2 tablespoons capers, drained
2 tablespoons balsamic vinegar
3 cloves garlic, minced
1 teaspoon dried oregano leaves
¼ teaspoon salt
⅓ cup packed fresh basil, cut into thin strips
  Toasted sliced Italian or French bread

Slow Cooker Directions

1. Mix eggplant, tomatoes, onion, bell pepper, salsa, oil, capers, vinegar, garlic, oregano and salt in slow cooker.

2. Cover; cook on LOW 7 to 8 hours or until vegetables are crisp-tender.

3. Stir in basil. Serve at room temperature on toasted bread.

Makes about 5¼ cups or 10 to 12 servings

tip

Not everything on the appetizer table needs to be homemade. A small wheel of cheese, specialty crackers and cocktail breads, cut-up raw vegetables from the deli, grapes, salsa and chips, and hummus are excellent additions to your menu.

Caponata

Pesto Chicken-Fontina Crostini

1 baguette, cut into 30 (¼-inch-thick) slices
½ (16-ounce) package PERDUE® Fit N Easy® Thin Sliced Skinless &
Boneless Chicken Breast or Turkey Breast Cutlets, cut into
30 pieces (8 ounces)
1 tablespoon prepared pesto
¼ teaspoon red pepper flakes
6 ounces fontina, cut into 30 pieces
½ cup roasted red peppers, cut into 1-inch pieces
30 small fresh basil leaves to garnish

Preheat oven to 400°F. Place baguette slices on a baking sheet and toast until golden.

Spray a nonstick skillet with olive oil cooking spray and warm over high heat. Add chicken and sauté until firm and golden. Stir in pesto and red pepper flakes. Set aside.

Place a piece of fontina on each baguette slice and return to oven until cheese melts. Top each crostini with a piece of chicken and a piece of roasted pepper. Garnish with basil leaves and serve.   *Makes 30 appetizers or 10 servings*

Prep Time: 30 minutes
Cook Time: 10 minutes

Ham Spirals

1 (3-ounce) package cream cheese, softened
¼ cup finely chopped dried tart cherries
3 tablespoons finely chopped pecans
2 tablespoons mayonnaise
½ teaspoon honey mustard or spicy brown mustard
4 thin slices cooked ham

Combine cream cheese, dried cherries, pecans, mayonnaise and mustard in small bowl; mix well.

Spread cherry mixture evenly on ham slices. Roll up jelly-roll style; fasten with wooden picks. Let chill several hours. Remove wooden picks. Slice each ham roll crosswise into ¼-inch slices; serve with crackers.   *Makes about 40 pieces or 10 servings*

Favorite recipe from **Cherry Marketing Institute**

Spicy Beef Turnovers

½ pound 90% lean ground beef or turkey
2 cloves garlic, minced
2 tablespoons soy sauce
1 tablespoon water
½ teaspoon cornstarch
1 teaspoon curry powder
¼ teaspoon Chinese five-spice powder*
¼ teaspoon red pepper flakes
2 tablespoons minced green onion
1 package (7½ ounces) refrigerated biscuits
1 egg
1 tablespoon water

Chinese five-spice powder is a blend of cinnamon, cloves, fennel seed, anise and Szechuan peppercorns. It is available in most supermarkets and at Asian grocery stores.

1. Preheat oven to 400°F. Lightly coat baking sheet with nonstick cooking spray; set aside. Cook beef with garlic in medium skillet over medium-high heat until beef is no longer pink, stirring to separate beef. Spoon off fat.

2. Stir soy sauce and water into cornstarch in cup until smooth. Add soy sauce mixture, curry powder, five-spice powder and red pepper flakes to skillet. Cook and stir 30 seconds or until liquid is absorbed. Remove from heat; stir in onion.

3. Roll each biscuit between 2 sheets of waxed paper into 4-inch rounds. Spoon heaping tablespoon beef mixture onto one side of each biscuit; fold over, forming a semi-circle. Pinch edges together to seal.**

4. Arrange turnovers on prepared baking sheet. Beat egg with water in cup; brush lightly over turnovers. Bake 9 to 10 minutes or until golden brown. Serve warm or at room temperature. *Makes 10 appetizers*

**At this point, turnovers may be wrapped and frozen up to 3 months. Thaw completely before proceeding as directed in step 4.*

Beef, Pork & Lamb

Slow-Cooked Korean Beef Short Ribs

    4 to 4½ pounds beef short ribs
    ¼ cup chopped green onions with tops
    ¼ cup tamari or soy sauce
    ¼ cup beef broth or water
    1 tablespoon brown sugar
    2 teaspoons minced fresh ginger
    2 teaspoons minced garlic
    ½ teaspoon black pepper
    2 teaspoons dark sesame oil
    Hot cooked rice or linguini pasta
    2 teaspoons sesame seeds, toasted

Slow Cooker Directions

1. Place ribs in slow cooker. Combine green onions, tamari, broth, brown sugar, ginger, garlic and pepper in medium bowl; mix well and pour over ribs. Cover; cook on LOW 7 to 8 hours or until ribs are fork tender.

2. Remove ribs from cooking liquid; cool slightly. Trim excess fat. Cut rib meat into bite-size pieces discarding bones and fat.

3. Let cooking liquid stand 5 minutes to allow fat to rise. Skim off fat.

4. Stir sesame oil into liquid. Return beef to slow cooker. Cover; cook on LOW 15 to 30 minutes or until hot.

5. Serve with rice; garnish with sesame seeds. *Makes 6 servings*

Prep Time: 10 to 15 minutes
Cook Time: 7 to 8 hours

Slow-Cooked Korean Beef Short Ribs

Barbara's Pork Chop Dinner

1 tablespoon butter
1 tablespoon olive oil
6 pork loin chops
1 can (10¾ ounces) condensed cream of chicken soup, undiluted
1 can (4 ounces) mushrooms, drained and chopped
¼ cup Dijon mustard
¼ cup chicken broth
2 cloves garlic, minced
½ teaspoon salt
½ teaspoon dried basil leaves
¼ teaspoon black pepper
6 red potatoes, unpeeled, cut into thin slices
1 onion, sliced
Chopped fresh parsley

Slow Cooker Directions

1. Heat butter and oil in large skillet. Brown pork chops on both sides. Set aside.

2. Combine soup, mushrooms, mustard, chicken broth, garlic, salt, basil and pepper in slow cooker. Add potatoes and onion, stirring to coat. Place pork chops on top of potato mixture.

3. Cover; cook on LOW 8 to 10 hours or on HIGH 4 to 5 hours. Sprinkle with parsley just before serving.   *Makes 6 servings*

tip

This recipe proves that you can have a busy day and still have time to entertain. Start the slow cooker in the morning and at the last minute, roast bell pepper slices tossed with olive oil in a preheated 425°F oven for 20 minutes or until they are tender. Add a salad of mixed greens and a dessert of ice cream topped with fresh fruit.

Barbara's Pork Chop Dinner

Lasagna Supreme

8 ounces uncooked lasagna noodles
½ pound ground beef
½ pound mild Italian sausage, casings removed
1 medium onion, chopped
2 cloves garlic, minced
1 can (14½ ounces) whole peeled tomatoes, undrained and chopped
1 can (6 ounces) tomato paste
2 teaspoons dried basil leaves
1 teaspoon dried marjoram leaves
1 can (4 ounces) sliced mushrooms, drained
2 eggs
2 cups (16 ounces) cream-style cottage cheese
¾ cup grated Parmesan cheese, divided
2 tablespoons dried parsley flakes
½ teaspoon salt
½ teaspoon black pepper
2 cups (8 ounces) shredded Cheddar cheese
3 cups (12 ounces) shredded mozzarella cheese

1. Cook lasagna noodles according to package directions; drain.

2. Cook meats, onion and garlic in large skillet over medium-high heat until meat is brown, stirring to separate meat. Drain drippings from skillet.

3. Add tomatoes with juice, tomato paste, basil and marjoram. Reduce heat to low. Cover; simmer 15 minutes, stirring often. Stir in mushrooms; set aside.

4. Preheat oven to 375°F. Beat eggs in large bowl; add cottage cheese, ½ cup Parmesan cheese, parsley, salt and pepper. Mix well.

5. Place half the noodles in bottom of greased 13×9-inch baking pan. Spread half the cottage cheese mixture over noodles, then half the meat mixture and half the Cheddar cheese and mozzarella cheese. Repeat layers. Sprinkle with remaining ¼ cup Parmesan cheese.

6. Bake lasagna 40 to 45 minutes or until bubbly. Let stand 10 minutes before cutting. *Makes 8 to 10 servings*

Tip: Lasagna can be assembled, covered and refrigerated up to 2 days in advance. Bake, uncovered, in preheated 375°F oven 60 minutes or until bubbly.

Lasagna Supreme

Stuffed Flank Steak

1 cup dry red wine
¼ cup soy sauce
2 cloves garlic, minced
1 large flank steak, 1½ to 2 pounds
1 cup thawed frozen chopped spinach, squeezed dry
1 jar (7 ounces) roasted red bell peppers, drained and chopped
½ cup crumbled blue cheese
Salt and black pepper

1. Combine wine, soy sauce and garlic in small bowl. Place steak in large resealable plastic food storage bag; pour marinade over steak. Seal bag; marinate in refrigerator 2 hours.

2. Preheat oven to 350°F. Combine spinach, roasted peppers and cheese in medium bowl. Remove steak from marinade, reserving marinade. Pat steak dry and place on flat work surface.

3. Spoon spinach mixture lengthwise across ⅔ of steak. Roll steak tightly around vegetables, securing with toothpicks or string.

4. Season with salt and black pepper; place in roasting pan, seam side down. Bake 30 to 40 minutes for medium-rare, or until desired degree of doneness is reached, basting twice with reserved marinade. Do not baste during last 10 minutes of cooking time. Allow steak to rest about 10 minutes before slicing.   *Makes 6 servings*

Serving Suggestion: Serve with steamed green beans and Vegetable Couscous (page 213).

Stuffed Flank Steak

Herbed Lamb Chops

⅓ **cup vegetable oil**
⅓ **cup red wine vinegar**
2 **tablespoons soy sauce**
1 **tablespoon lemon juice**
3 **cloves garlic, crushed**
1 **teaspoon salt**
1 **teaspoon chopped fresh oregano** *or* ¼ **teaspoon dried oregano**
    leaves
1 **teaspoon dried rosemary leaves**
1 **teaspoon dry mustard**
½ **teaspoon white pepper**
8 **lamb loin chops (about 2 pounds), 1 inch thick**

1. Combine all ingredients except chops in large resealable plastic food storage bag. Reserve ½ cup marinade for basting. Add chops; seal bag. Marinate in refrigerator at least 1 hour.

2. Remove chops from marinade; discard used marinade. Grill or broil chops about 8 minutes or until desired doneness, turning once and basting often with reserved ½ cup marinade. Discard any remaining marinade.   *Makes 4 to 6 servings*

Serving Suggestion: Serve with mashed potatoes and fresh green beans.

Herbed Lamb Chops

Double Cheese Veal Cutlets

2 tablespoons butter
1 pound veal cutlets
   Salt and black pepper
4 cups CLAMATO® Tomato Cocktail
   Pinch of dried thyme
2 tablespoons grated Parmesan cheese
1 cup (4 ounces) shredded Swiss cheese
1 avocado, peeled and sliced

1. In large skillet, melt butter. Brown cutlets a few at a time, 2 minutes on each side. Remove and sprinkle lightly with salt and pepper.

2. Return veal to skillet, overlapping cutlets. Add Clamato and thyme; simmer 5 to 10 minutes, or until veal is tender. Arrange veal in ovenproof serving dish and pour sauce over veal. Sprinkle with Parmesan cheese and Swiss cheese. Place under preheated broiler 5 minutes, or until cheese is melted. Top cutlets with avocado slices.

Makes 6 to 8 servings

Blueberry-Onion Sauced Pork Tenderloin

¾ to 1 pound pork tenderloin
2 tablespoons butter
2 medium onions, sliced
½ teaspoon salt
¼ teaspoon ground black pepper
2 tablespoons sugar
¼ cup port wine or sweet sherry
2 tablespoons balsamic vinegar
1 cup fresh or frozen blueberries
1 cup chopped cherry tomatoes

Preheat broiler. Broil pork, turning occasionally, until cooked through, about 20 minutes. Remove to a platter; cover to keep warm. Meanwhile, in a large skillet over medium-high heat, melt butter. Add onions, salt and pepper; cook until onions are golden, about 10 minutes. Add sugar; cook until onions are caramelized, 3 minutes longer. Add port, balsamic vinegar, blueberries and tomatoes; bring to a boil. Remove from heat. Thinly slice pork and serve with sauce.

Makes 4 servings

Favorite recipe from **US Highbush Blueberry Council**

Double Cheese Veal Cutlets

Muffin Stuffed Pork Chops

4 BAYS® English Muffins, split, lightly toasted
8 tablespoons butter or margarine, divided
1 cup finely chopped onion
1 cup finely chopped celery
¼ cup chopped walnuts
½ cup dried cranberries, chopped
1 teaspoon rubbed sage
4 center cut rib pork chops, 1 to 1¼ inch thick (8 to 10 ounces each)
Salt and pepper to taste
¾ cup chicken stock or broth
2 tablespoons Madeira or Port, divided
1 tablespoon heavy cream

Cut muffins into ¼-inch cubes. Melt 7 tablespoons butter in a skillet. Sauté onion, celery and walnuts over medium high heat until onion is softened. Stir in muffin cubes, cranberries and sage, stirring to coat evenly. Remove from heat.

With a sharp paring knife, cut a pocket in each chop all the way to rib. Sprinkle inside pockets with a little salt and pepper. Fill each pocket with about ⅓ cup stuffing and fasten together with wooden pick. Moisten remaining stuffing with ⅓ to ½ cup chicken stock and transfer to 1-quart casserole. Cover and bake in preheated 350°F oven for 30 minutes. Uncover and bake an additional 10 to 15 minutes.

Wipe out skillet. Heat remaining 1 tablespoon butter in skillet over low heat. Brown chops on both sides, about 5 minutes per side. Place in baking pan. Add chicken stock and 1 tablespoon Madeira to skillet and scrape up brown bits. Pour over chops, cover with foil and bake at 350°F for 40 to 45 minutes until meat is tender when pierced with tip of knife.

When chops are baked, remove to platter and keep warm. Strain drippings into glass measuring cup and spoon off fat. In a saucepan, boil drippings until reduced by half. Stir in remaining 1 tablespoon Madeira and cream. Boil until desired consistency. Spoon glaze over chops.

Makes 4 servings

Serving Suggestion: Serve Muffin Stuffed Pork Chops with sautéed apple rings and garlic mashed potatoes.

Muffin Stuffed Pork Chop

Italian Tomato Bake

1 pound sweet Italian sausage, cut into ½-inch slices
2 tablespoons margarine or butter
1 cup chopped onion
4 cups cooked egg noodles
2 cups frozen broccoli florets, thawed and drained
2 cups prepared pasta sauce
½ cup diced plum tomatoes
2 cloves garlic, minced
3 plum tomatoes, sliced
1 cup (8 ounces) low-fat ricotta cheese
⅓ cup grated Parmesan cheese
1 teaspoon dried oregano leaves

1. Preheat oven to 350°F. Cook sausage in large skillet over medium heat about 10 minutes or until barely pink in center. Drain on paper towels; set aside. Drain fat from skillet.

2. Add margarine and onion to skillet; cook and stir until onion is tender. Combine onion, noodles, broccoli, pasta sauce, diced tomatoes and garlic in large bowl; mix well. Transfer to 13×9-inch baking dish.

3. Top with sausage; arrange tomato slices on top. Place 1 heaping tablespoonful ricotta cheese on each tomato slice. Sprinkle casserole with Parmesan cheese and oregano. Bake 35 minutes or until hot and bubbly. *Makes 6 servings*

tip

This casserole is a perfect choice for a buffet dinner—it looks beautiful and it tastes delicious. Plus, it can be assembled early in the day, covered and refrigerated. Add 20 minutes to the baking time. When you include it on the buffet with an assortment of main and side dishes, it will serve twelve.

Italian Tomato Bake

Braciola

1 can (28 ounces) tomato sauce
2½ teaspoons dried oregano leaves, divided
1¼ teaspoons dried basil leaves, divided
1 teaspoon salt
½ pound bulk hot Italian sausage
½ cup chopped onion
¼ cup grated Parmesan cheese
2 cloves garlic, minced
1 tablespoon dried parsley flakes
1 to 2 beef flank steaks (about 2½ pounds)

Slow Cooker Directions

1. Combine tomato sauce, 2 teaspoons oregano, 1 teaspoon basil and salt in medium bowl; set aside.

2. Cook sausage in large nonstick skillet over medium-high heat until no longer pink, stirring to separate; drain well. Combine sausage, onion, cheese, garlic, parsley, remaining ½ teaspoon oregano and ¼ teaspoon basil in medium bowl; set aside.

3. Place steak on countertop between two pieces waxed paper. Pound with meat mallet until steak is ⅛ to ¼ inch thick. Cut steak into about 3-inch-wide strips.

4. Spoon sausage mixture evenly onto each steak strip. Roll up, jelly-roll style, securing meat with toothpicks. Place each roll in slow cooker. Pour tomato sauce mixture over meat. Cover; cook on LOW 6 to 8 hours or until meat is tender.

5. Cut each roll into slices. Arrange slices on dinner plates. Top with tomato sauce.

Makes 8 servings

Prep Time: 35 minutes
Cook Time: 6 to 8 hours

Serving Suggestion: Serve with green beans, tossed salad and garlic bread.

Braciola

Ham and Swiss Quiche

1 *unbaked* **9-inch (4-cup volume) deep-dish pie shell**
1 cup (4 ounces) shredded Swiss cheese, *divided*
1 cup finely chopped cooked ham
2 green onions, sliced
1 can (12 fluid ounces) NESTLÉ® CARNATION® Evaporated Milk
3 eggs
¼ cup all-purpose flour
¼ teaspoon salt
⅛ teaspoon ground black pepper

PREHEAT oven to 350°F.

SPRINKLE ½ *cup* cheese, ham and green onions into pie crust. Whisk together evaporated milk, eggs, flour, salt and pepper in large bowl. Pour mixture into pie shell; sprinkle with *remaining* cheese.

BAKE for 45 to 50 minutes or until knife inserted near center comes out clean. Cool on wire rack for 10 minutes before serving.   *Makes 8 servings*

For Mini-Quiche Appetizers: Use 1½ packages (3 crusts) refrigerated pie crusts. Grease miniature muffin pans. Unfold crust on lightly floured surface. Cut fourteen 2½-inch circles from each crust. Press 1 circle of dough into bottom and up side of each cup. Repeat with *remaining* crusts. Combine cheese, ham, green onions, ⅔ cup *(5-fluid-ounce can)* evaporated milk, 2 eggs (lightly beaten), *2 tablespoons* flour, salt and pepper in large bowl; mix well. Spoon mixture into crusts, filling ¾ full. Bake in preheated 350°F. oven for 20 to 25 minutes or until crusts are golden brown. Cool slightly; lift quiche from cup with tip of knife. Serve warm or cool and freeze for later entertaining. Makes 3½ dozen.

Ham and Swiss Quiche

Shelby Slow Cooker Rouladen

12 slices top round beef, pounded thin (¼ inch thick)
Salt and black pepper
Garlic pepper
¼ cup Dijon mustard
1½ cups chopped onions
1½ cups chopped dill pickle
Nonstick cooking spray
¼ cup (½ stick) butter
5 tablespoons flour
2 cans (14½ ounces each) beef broth
1 pound peeled baby carrots
4 stalks celery, cut into 1-inch pieces

Slow Cooker Directions

1. Place 1 slice of beef on clean cutting board; season with salt, pepper and garlic pepper. Spread with about 1 teaspoon mustard; top with about 2 tablespoons *each* onion and pickle. Starting at short side of beef fold about ⅓ of slice over on itself, tuck in long sides, then roll tightly. Secure with toothpick. Repeat with remaining slices of beef, salt, pepper, garlic pepper, mustard, onions and pickles.

2. Spray large nonstick skillet with cooking spray. Brown rolled beef slices in batches over medium-high heat until browned on all sides. Remove from skillet.

3. In same skillet, melt butter. Sprinkle with flour; stir until a smooth paste forms. Add beef broth, stirring constantly. Cook and stir until mixture thickens.

4. Pour half of broth mixture into slow cooker. Add beef rolls; add remaining broth mixture. Top with carrots and celery.

5. Cover; cook on LOW 8 to 10 hours or on HIGH 4 to 5 hours or until beef is tender.

Makes 6 to 8 servings

Pork Chops with Shallot Stuffing

6 tablespoons Lucini Premium Select extra virgin olive oil, divided
1½ cups minced shallots (about 1 pound)*
1 tablespoon dried oregano leaves *or* 4 tablespoons chopped fresh oregano
1 cup white wine or chicken broth
2 cups (8 ounces) JARLSBERG cheese, shredded
8 (¾- to 1-inch-thick) loin pork chops with bone, pockets slit for bread stuffing (about 3½ to 4 pounds)
¼ cup all-purpose flour

Mincing can be done in a food processor. Pulse on and off to achieve a coarse consistency, not a purée.

In 2 tablespoons oil, cook shallots and oregano over medium heat, stirring until softened. Add wine and cook 5 minutes or until liquid is reduced by half.

Remove from heat and stir in cheese. Stuff mixture into pockets of pork chops, dividing stuffing evenly. Secure with wooden picks, if desired. Dredge chops lightly in flour.

Heat 2 tablespoons oil in each of 2 heavy skillets. Cook chops 4 minutes on first side over medium-high heat. Turn chops and cook second side over medium heat 6 minutes or until done. During cooking, if some stuffing comes out, tuck it back in with spatula.

Makes 8 servings

Serving Suggestion: Serve with noodles or brown rice, broccoli and warm crusty rolls.

Lamb Chops with Mustard Sauce

        1 teaspoon dried thyme leaves
    ½ teaspoon salt
    ¼ teaspoon black pepper
        4 (1½-inch-thick) center cut loin lamb chops (about 1½ pounds
            total)
        2 tablespoons canola or vegetable oil
    ¼ cup finely chopped shallots or sweet onion
    ¼ cup beef or chicken broth
        2 tablespoons Worcestershire sauce
    1½ tablespoons Dijon mustard
        Chopped fresh thyme (optional)

1. Sprinkle dried thyme, salt and pepper over lamb. Heat oil in large skillet over medium heat. Add chops; cook 4 minutes per side. Remove chops from skillet; set aside.

2. Add shallots to skillet; cook 3 minutes, stirring occasionally. Reduce heat to medium-low. Add broth, Worcestershire sauce and mustard; simmer 5 minutes or until sauce thickens slightly, stirring occasionally. Return chops to skillet; cook 2 minutes for medium-rare, turning once. Transfer to serving plates; top with fresh thyme, if desired.

Makes 4 servings

Mesquite & Garlic Grilled Steak

    1½ pounds beef steak, 1-inch thick (top sirloin, rib-eye or T-bone)
        1 bottle (12 ounces) LAWRY'S® Mesquite Marinade With Lime Juice
    1½ teaspoons LAWRY'S® Seasoned Pepper
        1 teaspoon LAWRY'S® Garlic Powder With Parsley

Place steak in large resealable plastic bag. In medium bowl, mix together Mesquite Marinade, Seasoned Pepper and Garlic Powder With Parsley; reserve ⅓ cup marinade mixture. Pour remaining marinade mixture into bag with steak; seal bag. Marinate in refrigerator for 30 minutes, turning once. Remove steak from bag, discarding used marinade. Grill, brushing often with reserved marinade mixture, until desired degree of doneness, about 16 to 20 minutes. *Makes 4 to 6 servings*

Prep Time: 7 minutes
Marinate Time: 30 minutes
Cook Time: 16 to 20 minutes

Lamb Chop with Mustard Sauce

Tenderloin Deluxe with Mushroom Sauce

10 tablespoons I CAN'T BELIEVE IT'S NOT BUTTER!® Spread, divided
¼ cup chopped green onions
1 tablespoon Dijon-style mustard
1 teaspoon soy sauce
1 (2½-to 3-pound) beef tenderloin
8 ounces mushrooms, sliced
2 medium onions, finely chopped
2 cloves garlic, finely chopped
⅓ cup dry sherry
4 drops hot pepper sauce
1 cup beef broth

Preheat oven to 425°F.

In small bowl, blend 4 tablespoons I Can't Believe It's Not Butter!® Spread, green onions, mustard and soy sauce. In 13×9-inch baking or roasting pan, arrange beef and evenly spread with mustard mixture.

Bake uncovered 15 minutes. *Reduce heat to 400°F* and bake 45 minutes or until desired doneness. Let stand 10 minutes before slicing.

Meanwhile, in 12-inch skillet, melt remaining 6 tablespoons I Can't Believe It's Not Butter!® Spread over medium-high heat and cook mushrooms, stirring occasionally, 3 minutes or until softened. Stir in onions and cook, stirring occasionally, 12 minutes or until golden brown. Add garlic and cook 30 seconds. Stir in sherry and hot pepper sauce and cook 2 minutes. Stir in broth and simmer 5 minutes or until sauce is slightly thickened. Serve sauce over sliced beef. *Makes 6 servings*

Tenderloin Deluxe with Mushroom Sauce

Apple Stuffed Pork Loin Roast

2 cloves garlic, minced
1 teaspoon coarse salt
1 teaspoon dried rosemary leaves
½ teaspoon dried thyme leaves
½ teaspoon freshly ground black pepper
1 boneless center cut pork loin roast (4 to 5 pounds)
1 tablespoon butter
2 large tart apples, peeled, cored and thinly sliced (2 cups)
1 medium onion, cut into thin strips (about 1 cup)
2 tablespoons brown sugar
1 teaspoon Dijon mustard
1 cup apple cider or apple juice

1. Preheat oven to 325°F. Combine garlic, salt, rosemary, thyme and pepper in small bowl. Butterfly roast, cutting lengthwise down roast almost to, but not through the bottom. Open like a book. Rub half garlic mixture onto cut sides of pork.

2. Melt butter in large skillet over medium-high heat. Add apples and onion; cook and stir 5 to 10 minutes or until soft. Stir in brown sugar and mustard. Spread mixture evenly on one cut side of roast. Close halves; tie roast with cotton string at 2-inch intervals. Place roast on rack in shallow roasting pan. Pour apple cider over roast. Rub outside of roast with remaining garlic mixture.

3. Roast, uncovered, basting frequently with pan drippings, 2 to 2½ hours or until instant-read thermometer inserted in the thickest part registers 155°F. Let roast stand for 15 minutes before slicing. The internal temperature will continue to rise 5°F to 10°F during stand time. Carve roast crosswise. *Makes 14 to 16 servings*

Serving Suggestion: Serve with broccoli or Brussels sprouts, buttered noodles tossed with grated Parmesan cheese, and a tomato and cucumber salad.

Apple Stuffed Pork Loin Roast

Chicken & Turkey

Chicken Tuscany

    6 medium red potatoes, scrubbed and sliced ⅛ inch thick
12 ounces shiitake, cremini, chanterelle and/or button mushrooms, sliced
    4 tablespoons olive oil, divided
    4 tablespoons grated Parmesan cheese, divided
    3 teaspoons minced garlic, divided
    3 teaspoons minced fresh rosemary *or* 1½ teaspoons dried rosemary leaves, divided
    Salt and ground pepper
    1 package (about 3 pounds) PERDUE® Fresh Pick of the Chicken

Preheat oven to 425°F. Pat potatoes dry with paper towels. Toss potatoes and mushrooms with 2½ tablespoons oil, 2 tablespoons cheese, 2 teaspoons garlic, 2 teaspoons rosemary, ½ teaspoon salt and ¼ teaspoon pepper. In 13×9-inch baking dish, arrange potatoes in one layer; top with remaining 2 tablespoons cheese. Bake 15 minutes or until potatoes are lightly browned; set aside.

Meanwhile, in large nonstick skillet over medium heat, heat remaining 1½ tablespoons oil. Add chicken pieces. Season lightly with salt and pepper; sprinkle with remaining 1 teaspoon rosemary and garlic. Cook chicken 5 to 6 minutes on each side or until browned. (Do not crowd pan; if necessary, brown chicken in two batches.)

Arrange chicken on top of potato mixture; drizzle with any oil from skillet and return to oven. Bake 20 to 25 minutes longer or until chicken is no longer pink in center. Serve chicken, potatoes and mushrooms with green salad, if desired.

Makes 6 servings

Chicken Tuscany

Chicken, Asparagus & Mushroom Bake

1 tablespoon butter
1 tablespoon olive oil
2 boneless skinless chicken breasts (about ½ pound), cut into
    bite-size pieces
2 cloves garlic, minced
1 cup sliced mushrooms
2 cups sliced asparagus
    Black pepper
1 package (about 6 ounces) corn bread stuffing mix
¼ cup dry white wine (optional)
1 can (14½ ounces) reduced-sodium chicken broth
1 can (10½ ounces) condensed low-sodium condensed cream of
    asparagus or cream of chicken soup, undiluted

1. Preheat oven to 350°F. Heat butter and oil in large skillet until butter is melted. Cook and stir chicken and garlic about 3 minutes over medium-high heat until chicken is no longer pink. Add mushrooms; cook and stir 2 minutes. Add asparagus; cook and stir about 5 minutes or until asparagus is crisp-tender. Season with pepper.

2. Transfer mixture to 2½-quart casserole or 6 small casseroles. Top with stuffing mix.

3. Add wine to skillet, if desired; cook and stir 1 minute over medium-high heat, scraping up any browned bits from bottom of skillet. Add broth and soup; cook and stir until well blended.

4. Pour broth mixture into casserole; mix well. Bake, uncovered, about 35 minutes (30 minutes for small casseroles) or until heated through and lightly browned.

Makes 6 servings

Serving Suggestion: Serve with tossed green green salad and sliced tomatoes.

Chicken, Asparagus & Mushroom Bake

Turkey with Pecan-Cherry Stuffing

1 fresh or frozen boneless turkey breast (about 3 to 4 pounds)
2 cups cooked rice
1/3 cup chopped pecans
1/3 cup dried cherries or cranberries
1 teaspoon poultry seasoning
1/4 cup peach, apricot or plum preserves
1 teaspoon Worcestershire sauce

Slow Cooker Directions

1. Thaw turkey breast, if frozen. Remove and discard skin. Cut slices three fourths of the way through turkey at 1-inch intervals.

2. Stir together rice, pecans, cherries and poultry seasoning in large bowl. Stuff rice mixture between slices. If needed, skewer turkey lengthwise to hold together.

3. Place turkey in large slow cooker. Cover; cook on LOW 5 to 6 hours or until turkey registers 170°F on meat thermometer inserted into thickest part of breast, not touching stuffing.

4. Stir together preserves and Worcestershire sauce. Spoon over turkey. Cover; let stand for 5 minutes. Remove and discard skewer, if used. *Makes 8 servings*

Prep Time: 20 minutes
Cook Time: 5 to 6 hours
Stand Time: 5 minutes

Serving Suggestion: Serve with asparagus spears, crescent rolls and spinach salad.

Turkey with Pecan-Cherry Stuffing

Chicken and Black Bean Enchiladas

2 jars (16 ounces each) mild picante sauce
¼ cup chopped fresh cilantro
2 tablespoons chili powder
1 teaspoon ground cumin
2 cups (10 ounces) chopped cooked chicken
1 can (15 ounces) black beans, drained and rinsed
1⅓ cups *French's*® French Fried Onions, divided
1 package (about 10 ounces) flour tortillas (7 inches)
1 cup (4 ounces) shredded Monterey Jack cheese with jalapeño peppers

Preheat oven to 350°F. Grease 15×10-inch jelly-roll baking pan. Combine picante sauce, cilantro, chili powder and cumin in large saucepan. Bring to a boil. Reduce heat to low; simmer 5 minutes.

Combine 1½ cups sauce mixture, chicken, beans and ⅔ cup French Fried Onions in medium bowl. Spoon a scant ½ cup filling over bottom third of each tortilla. Roll up tortillas enclosing filling and arrange, seam-side down, in a single layer in bottom of prepared baking pan. Spoon remaining sauce evenly over tortillas.

Bake, uncovered, 20 minutes or until heated through. Sprinkle with remaining ⅔ cup onions and cheese. Bake 5 minutes or until cheese is melted and onions are golden. Serve immediately.   *Makes 5 to 6 servings (4 cups sauce, 4½ cups filling)*

Tip: This is a great make-ahead party dish.

Prep Time: 45 minutes
Cook Time: 25 minutes

Chicken and Black Bean Enchiladas

Pineapple Turkey Kabobs

1½ pounds boneless skinless turkey tenders
2 large red bell peppers
2 cups fresh pineapple chunks
½ cup rice wine vinegar
¼ cup pickled ginger
2 teaspoons chopped garlic
½ teaspoon black pepper
Hot cooked brown or white rice (optional)

1. Soak 6 wooden skewers in water 20 minutes. Preheat oven to 400°F.

2. Wash and pat dry turkey tenders; cut into bite-size pieces. Place in resealable plastic food storage bag.

3. Cut bell peppers into quarters, then into bite-size chunks. Place in bag with turkey. Add pineapple, vinegar, pickled ginger, garlic and black pepper to bag with turkey. Seal bag, turn several times to coat all ingredients. Refrigerate 20 minutes.

4. Spray 12×8×2 baking pan with nonstick cooking spray. Alternately thread bell pepper, turkey, ginger and pineapple onto 6 skewers. Place in pan; cover with foil Bake 20 to 25 minutes. *Makes 6 servings*

Serving Suggestion: Serve with rice and torn fresh spinach, lightly sautéed in olive oil.

Pineapple Turkey Kabob

Sweet & Sour Chicken and Rice

1 pound chicken tenders
1 can (8 ounces) pineapple chunks, drained and juice reserved
1 cup uncooked rice
2 carrots, thinly sliced
1 green bell pepper, cut into 1-inch pieces
1 large onion, chopped
3 cloves garlic, minced
1 can (14½ ounces) reduced-sodium chicken broth
⅓ cup soy sauce
3 tablespoons sugar
3 tablespoons apple cider vinegar
1 tablespoon sesame oil
1½ teaspoons ground ginger
¼ cup chopped peanuts (optional)
Chopped fresh cilantro (optional)

1. Preheat oven to 350°F. Spray 13×9-inch baking dish with nonstick cooking spray.

2. Combine chicken, pineapple, rice, carrots, bell pepper, onion and garlic in prepared dish.

3. Place broth, reserved pineapple juice, soy sauce, sugar, vinegar, sesame oil and ginger in small saucepan; bring to a boil over high heat. Remove from heat and pour over chicken mixture.

4. Cover tightly with foil and bake 40 to 50 minutes or until chicken is no longer pink and rice is tender. Sprinkle with peanuts and cilantro, if desired.

Makes 6 servings

Sweet & Sour Chicken and Rice

Chicken Cassoulet

4 slices bacon
¼ cup all-purpose flour
Salt and black pepper
1¾ pounds chicken pieces
2 cooked chicken sausages, cut into ¼-inch pieces
1 onion, chopped
1½ cups diced red and green bell peppers (2 small bell peppers)
2 cloves garlic, finely chopped
1 teaspoon dried thyme leaves
Salt and black pepper
Olive oil
2 cans (about 15 ounces each) cannellini or Great Northern beans, rinsed and drained
½ cup dry white wine or chicken broth

1. Preheat oven to 350°F. Cook bacon in large skillet over medium-high heat until crisp. Remove and drain on paper towels. Cut into 1-inch pieces.

2. Pour off all but 2 tablespoons fat from skillet. Place flour in shallow bowl; season with salt and black pepper. Dip chicken pieces in flour mixture; shake off excess. Brown chicken in batches over medium-high heat in skillet; remove and set aside. Lightly brown sausages in same skillet; remove and set aside.

3. Add onion, bell peppers, garlic, thyme, salt and black pepper to skillet. Cook and stir over medium heat about 5 minutes or until softened, adding olive oil as needed to prevent sticking. Transfer onion mixture to 13×9-inch baking dish. Add beans; mix well. Top with chicken, sausages and bacon. Add wine to skillet; cook and stir over medium heat, scraping up brown bits on bottom of pan. Pour over casserole.

4. Cover; bake 40 minutes. Uncover and bake 15 minutes more or until chicken is no longer pink in center and juices run clear.   *Makes 6 servings*

Chicken Cassoulet

California Chicken Pot Pies

1 (9-inch) folded refrigerated unbaked pie crust
1 can (10¾ ounces) condensed cream of chicken soup
1 cup half 'n' half or milk
2 cups (10 ounces) cooked chicken, cut into ½-inch cubes
1 bag (16 ounces) California-style frozen vegetable combination, such as cauliflower, carrots and asparagus, thawed and drained*
1⅓ cups *French's*® French Fried Onions, divided
¼ teaspoon dried thyme leaves
½ cup (2 ounces) shredded Swiss cheese

Or, substitute any package of combination vegetables for California-style vegetables.

Preheat oven to 400°F. Roll out pie crust onto lightly floured board. Invert 10-ounce custard cup on top of crust. With sharp knife, trace around cup and cut out circle; prick several times with fork. Repeat 5 more times, rerolling scraps of pie crust as necessary. Cover; set crusts aside.

Combine soup and half 'n' half in large bowl. Stir in chicken, vegetables, ⅔ cup French Fried Onions and thyme. Spoon mixture evenly into 6 (10-ounce) custard cups. Place filled cups on baking sheet. Place 1 crust over each cup. Bake, uncovered, 30 minutes or until crust is browned.

Sprinkle crusts with cheese; top with remaining ⅔ cup onions. Bake 1 minute or until onions are golden.   *Makes 6 servings*

Note: Filling may be baked in 9-inch pie plate. Top with uncut 9-inch pie crust. Bake at 400°F 35 minutes or until crust is golden. Top with cheese and remaining ⅔ cup onions. Bake 1 minute or until onions are golden.

Make-Ahead Tips: Pot pies may be prepared ahead, baked and frozen. Do not top with cheese and remaining onions before freezing. To reheat: Microwave individual pies in microwavable dishes on HIGH 5 minutes or until heated through. Top with remaining cheese and ⅔ cup onions. Microwave 1 minute or until onions are golden. Or, prepare pies as above. Do not bake. Cover; freeze. Bake at 400°F 40 minutes or until heated through and crust is golden. Top with cheese and remaining ⅔ cup onions. Bake 1 minute.

Prep Time: 15 minutes
Cook Time: 31 minutes

California Chicken Pot Pies

Lemon Rosemary Roast Chicken

1 whole chicken (about 4 to 4½ pounds)
2½ teaspoons LAWRY'S® Seasoned Salt
2 teaspoons whole dried rosemary, crumbled
1 teaspoon LAWRY'S® Lemon Pepper

Rinse chicken with cold water; pat dry with paper towels. In small bowl, combine Seasoned Salt, rosemary and Lemon Pepper. Gently lift skin from meat on breast. Rub seasoning mixture onto meat under skin, all over outside of chicken and inside cavity. Place chicken, breast-side-up, in 13×9×2-inch baking dish. Roast in 400°F oven for 60 minutes or until meat thermometer inserted in thickest part of chicken thigh reaches 180°F. Let stand 10 minutes before carving. *Makes 8 servings*

Hint: Loosely 'crunch up' some foil in the baking dish around the chicken to keep grease from splattering in the oven. Also, elevate the chicken on a cooling rack in the dish to help brown the bottom of the chicken.

Prep Time: 10 minutes
Cook Time: 60 to 70 minutes

Roast Chicken & Kiwifruit with Raspberry Glaze

2 chickens, quartered (3½ to 4 pounds each)
1 teaspoon salt
¼ teaspoon black pepper
2 tablespoons butter or margarine, melted
Raspberry Glaze (recipe follows)
2 kiwifruit, peeled and sliced

Preheat oven to 400°F. Sprinkle chicken with salt and pepper. Place, skin side up, in single layer in large, shallow pan; brush with butter. Roast, basting frequently with butter, about 45 minutes or until chicken is tender and juices run clear. Drain off fat. While chicken is roasting, prepare Raspberry Glaze. Spoon glaze over chicken; top with kiwifruit slices. Spoon glaze from bottom of pan over chicken and kiwifruit. Bake about 5 minutes, basting frequently with pan juices, or until kiwifruit and chicken are well glazed. *Makes 8 servings*

Raspberry Glaze: Combine 1 cup seedless raspberry preserves, ½ cup white port wine and grated peel of 1 lemon in small saucepan. Cook over low heat about 5 minutes or until slightly thickened.

*Favorite recipe from **Delmarva Poultry Industry, Inc.***

Lemon Rosemary Roast Chicken

Chicken Cacciatore

4 pounds chicken pieces
½ teaspoon salt, divided
¼ teaspoon black pepper, divided
1 tablespoon olive oil
1 medium onion, chopped
2 medium red or green bell peppers, cut into strips
2 cups sliced mushrooms
1 clove garlic, minced
1 can (28 ounces) whole tomatoes, undrained
½ cup dry red wine
2 teaspoons dried basil leaves
1 teaspoon dried oregano leaves
1 cup shredded part-skim mozzarella cheese
¼ cup grated Parmesan cheese
   Hot cooked spaghetti (optional)

1. Rinse chicken and pat dry with paper towels. Sprinkle with ¼ teaspoon salt and half the black pepper. Heat oil in deep 12-inch skillet over medium heat. Brown chicken on both sides; remove from skillet to plate.

2. Cook and stir onion 3 minutes. Add bell peppers, mushrooms and garlic. Cook and stir 3 to 4 minutes or until vegetables are softened. Cut tomatoes into quarters. Add tomatoes with juice, wine, basil, oregano, remaining ¼ teaspoon salt and black pepper. Bring to a boil.

3. Add chicken. Reduce heat to low. Cover and cook 25 to 30 minutes or until chicken juices run clear. Remove chicken from skillet; keep warm. Cook tomato mixture, uncovered, over medium heat 5 to 10 minutes or until tomato mixture thickens slightly. Return chicken to skillet; sprinkle with cheeses. Cook briefly until mozzarella cheese melts. Serve with hot cooked spaghetti, if desired.

Makes 6 servings

Chicken Cacciatore

Italian Chicken with Sausage & Peppers

2½ pounds chicken pieces
2 tablespoons olive oil
½ to ¾ pounds sweet Italian sausage
2 green bell peppers, chopped
1 onion, chopped
1 carrot, finely chopped
2 cloves garlic, minced
1 can (19 ounces) condensed tomato soup, undiluted
1 can (15 ounces) tomato sauce
¼ teaspoon dried oregano leaves
¼ teaspoon dried basil leaves
1 bay leaf
Salt and pepper

Slow Cooker Directions

1. Rinse chicken; pat dry. Heat oil in large skillet over medium-high heat. Cook chicken, skin side down, about 10 minutes, turning to brown both sides. Remove from skillet; set aside.

2. In same skillet, cook sausage 4 to 5 minutes or until browned. Remove from skillet. Cut into 1-inch pieces; set aside. Drain off all but 1 tablespoon fat from skillet.

3. Add bell peppers, onion, carrot and garlic to skillet. Cook 4 to 5 minutes or until vegetables are tender.

4. Add tomato soup, tomato sauce, oregano, basil and bay leaf; stir well. Season with salt and pepper. Transfer to slow cooker.

5. Add chicken and sausage to slow cooker. Cover; cook on LOW 6 to 8 hours or on HIGH 4 to 6 hours. Remove and discard bay leaf before serving.

Makes 6 servings

Italian Chicken with Sausage & Peppers

Chicken-Asparagus Casserole

2 teaspoons vegetable oil
1 cup seeded and chopped green and/or red bell peppers
1 medium onion, chopped
2 cloves garlic, minced
1 can (10¾ ounces) condensed cream of asparagus soup, undiluted
1 container (8 ounces) ricotta cheese
2 cups (8 ounces) shredded Cheddar cheese, divided
2 eggs
1½ cups chopped cooked chicken
1 package (10 ounces) frozen chopped asparagus,* thawed and drained
8 ounces egg noodles, cooked
Black pepper (optional)

*Or, substitute ½ pound fresh asparagus cut into ½-inch pieces. Bring 6 cups water to a boil over high heat in large saucepan. Add fresh asparagus. Reduce heat to medium. Cover and cook 5 to 8 minutes or until crisp-tender. Drain.

1. Preheat oven to 350°F. Grease 13×9-inch casserole; set aside.

2. Heat oil in small skillet over medium heat. Add bell peppers, onion and garlic; cook and stir until vegetables are crisp-tender.

3. Mix soup, ricotta cheese, 1 cup Cheddar cheese and eggs in large bowl until well blended. Add onion mixture, chicken, asparagus and noodles; mix well. Season with pepper, if desired.

4. Spread mixture evenly in prepared casserole. Top with remaining 1 cup Cheddar cheese.

5. Bake 30 minutes or until center is set and cheese is bubbly. Let stand 5 minutes before serving. Garnish as desired. *Makes 12 servings*

Chicken-Asparagus Casserole

Roasted Chicken au Jus

1 envelope LIPTON® RECIPE SECRETS® Onion Soup Mix*
2 tablespoons BERTOLLI® Olive Oil
1 (2½- to 3-pound) chicken, cut into serving pieces
½ cup hot water

Also terrific with LIPTON® RECIPE SECRETS® Savory Herb with Garlic, Onion Mushroom or Ranch Soup Mix.

1. Preheat oven to 425°F. In large bowl, combine soup mix and oil; add chicken and toss until evenly coated.

2. In bottom of broiler pan without rack, arrange chicken. Roast chicken, basting occasionally, 40 minutes or until chicken is thoroughly cooked.

3. Remove chicken to serving platter. Add hot water to pan and stir, scraping brown bits from bottom of pan. Serve sauce over chicken.   *Makes 4 servings*

Slow Cooker Method: Rub chicken pieces with soup mix combined with oil. Place chicken in slow cooker. Cover. Cook on HIGH 4 hours or LOW 6 to 8 hours. Serve as above.

The Original Ranch® Tetrazzini

8 ounces linguine, cooked and drained
3 cups shredded cooked chicken
1½ cups prepared HIDDEN VALLEY® The Original Ranch® Dressing
½ cup dry white wine or chicken broth
1 jar (4½ ounces) sliced mushrooms, drained
¼ cup buttered* bread crumbs

Melt 1½ teaspoons butter; stir in plain dry bread crumbs until evenly coated.

Combine linguine, chicken, dressing, wine and mushrooms. Pour into a 2-quart casserole dish. Top with crumbs. Bake at 350°F for 20 minutes or until bubbly around edges.   *Makes 6 servings*

Roasted Chicken au Jus

Fish & Shellfish

Shrimp Creole

> **2 tablespoons olive oil**
> **1½ cups chopped green bell pepper**
> **1 medium onion, chopped**
> **⅔ cup chopped celery**
> **2 cloves garlic, finely chopped**
> **1 cup uncooked rice**
> **1 can (about 14 ounces) diced tomatoes, drained and juice reserved**
> **1 teaspoon dried oregano leaves**
> **¾ teaspoon salt**
> **½ teaspoon dried thyme leaves**
> **2 teaspoons hot pepper sauce, or to taste**
>   **Black pepper**
> **1 pound raw medium shrimp, peeled and deveined**
> **1 tablespoon chopped fresh parsley (optional)**

1. Preheat oven to 325°F. Heat olive oil in large skillet over medium-high heat. Add bell pepper, onion, celery and garlic; cook and stir 5 minutes or until vegetables are soft.

2. Add rice; cook and stir 5 minutes over medium heat until rice is opaque. Add tomatoes, oregano, salt, thyme, hot sauce and black pepper to skillet; stir until blended. Pour reserved tomato juice into measuring cup. Add enough water to measure 1¾ cups liquid; add to skillet. Cook and stir 2 minutes.

3. Transfer mixture to 2½-quart casserole. Stir in shrimp. Bake, covered, 55 minutes or until rice is tender and liquid is absorbed. Sprinkle with fresh parsley, if desired.

Makes 4 to 6 servings

Shrimp Creole

Crab-Artichoke Casserole

8 ounces uncooked small shell pasta
2 tablespoons butter
6 green onions, chopped
2 tablespoons all-purpose flour
1 cup half-and-half
1 teaspoon dry mustard
½ teaspoon ground red pepper
   Salt and black pepper
½ cup (2 ounces) shredded Swiss cheese, divided
1 package (about 8 ounces) imitation crabmeat chunks
1 can (about 14 ounces) artichoke hearts, drained and cut into
    bite-size pieces

1. Preheat oven to 350°F. Grease 2-quart casserole. Cook pasta according to package directions; drain and set aside.

2. Melt butter in large saucepan over medium heat; add green onions. Cook and stir about 2 minutes. Add flour; cook and stir 2 minutes more. Gradually add half-and-half, whisking constantly until mixture begins to thicken. Whisk in mustard and red pepper; season to taste with salt and black pepper. Remove from heat and stir in ¼ cup cheese until melted.

3. Combine crabmeat, artichokes and pasta in casserole. Add sauce mixture and stir until well blended. Top with remaining ¼ cup cheese. Bake about 40 minutes or until hot, bubbly and lightly browned. *Makes 6 servings*

tip

You may substitute 8 ounces of fresh lump crabmeat or 2 (6-ounce) cans of crabmeat, drained, for the imitation crabmeat in this recipe.

Crab-Artichoke Casserole

Blackened Catfish

Easy Tartar Sauce (recipe follows)
4 (4-ounce) catfish fillets
2 teaspoons lemon juice
Nonstick garlic-flavored cooking spray
2 teaspoons blackened or Cajun seasoning blend
1 cup hot cooked rice

1. Prepare Easy Tartar Sauce.

2. Rinse catfish and pat dry with paper towel. Sprinkle with lemon juice; coat with cooking spray. Sprinkle with seasoning blend; coat again with cooking spray.

3. Heat large nonstick skillet over medium-high heat until hot. Add 2 fillets to skillet seasoned side down. Cook 3 minutes per side. Reduce heat to medium and cook 3 minutes more or until fish begins to flake when tested with a fork. Remove fillets from skillet; keep warm. Repeat with remaining fillets. Serve with tartar sauce and rice. *Makes 4 servings*

Easy Tartar Sauce: Combine ¼ cup mayonnaise, 2 tablespoons sweet pickle relish and 1 teaspoon lemon juice; mix well.

Spicy Fish Fillets with Lemon

Grated peel of ½ SUNKIST® lemon
1 teaspoon toasted sesame seeds
¼ teaspoon onion salt
⅛ teaspoon *each* ground cumin, white pepper and paprika
⅛ teaspoon red pepper flakes (optional)
4 tilapia or sole fillets (¾ pound)
1 tablespoon vegetable oil
Fresh SUNKIST® lemon wedges

In small bowl, combine lemon peel, sesame seeds, onion salt and spices. Rub into both sides of fish fillets. Heat oil in large nonstick skillet sprayed with nonstick cooking spray. Sauté fish over medium-high heat 3 minutes; turn and cook 2 to 3 minutes longer or until fish is opaque and flakes easily with fork. Serve with lemon wedges and garnish with parsley sprigs, if desired. *Makes 2 to 4 servings*

Blackened Catfish

Asian Honey-Tea Grilled Prawns

1½ pounds medium shrimp, peeled and deveined
   Salt
2 green onions, thinly sliced

Marinade
   1 cup brewed double-strength orange-spice tea, cooled
   ¼ cup honey
   ¼ cup rice vinegar
   ¼ cup soy sauce
   1 tablespoon fresh ginger, peeled and finely chopped
   ½ teaspoon ground black pepper

In plastic bag, combine marinade ingredients. Remove ½ cup marinade; set aside for dipping sauce. Add shrimp to marinade in bag, turning to coat. Close bag securely and marinate in refrigerator 30 minutes or up to 12 hours.

Remove shrimp from marinade; discard marinade. Thread shrimp onto 8 skewers, dividing evenly. Grill over medium coals 4 to 6 minutes or until shrimp turn pink and are just firm to the touch, turning once. Season with salt, as desired.

Meanwhile prepare dipping sauce by placing reserved ½ cup marinade in small saucepan. Bring to a boil over medium-high heat. Boil 3 to 5 minutes or until slightly reduced. Stir in green onions. *Makes 4 servings*

*Favorite recipe from **National Honey Board***

Serving Suggestion: Serve with rice and Sautéed Snow Peas & Baby Carrots (page 216).

Asian Honey-Tea Grilled Prawns

Baltimore Crab Cakes

16 ounces lump crabmeat, picked over and flaked
1 cup saltine cracker crumbs, divided
2 eggs, lightly beaten
¼ cup chopped green onions
¼ cup minced fresh parsley
¼ cup mayonnaise
2 tablespoons fresh lemon juice
1 teaspoon green pepper sauce
¼ teaspoon salt
Black pepper
4 tablespoons vegetable oil
2 tablespoons butter
Lemon wedges

1. Combine crabmeat, ¼ cup cracker crumbs, eggs, green onions, parsley, mayonnaise, lemon juice, pepper sauce, salt and pepper to taste in medium bowl; mix well. Shape mixture into 12 cakes, using ¼ cup crab mixture for each.

2. Place remaining ¾ cup cracker crumbs in shallow bowl. Coat crab cakes with crumb mixture, lightly pressing crumbs into cakes. Place cakes on plate; cover and refrigerate 30 minutes to 1 hour.

3. Heat oil and butter in large skillet over medium heat until butter is melted. Cook crab cakes 3 to 4 minutes until golden brown on bottoms. Turn and cook 3 minutes until golden brown and internal temperature reaches 170°F. Serve immediately with lemon wedges. *Makes 6 servings (2 crab cakes each)*

tip

To prepare 24 appetizer crab cakes, use 2 tablespoons crab mixture for each cake. Cook for 2 minutes per side. To make crab cakes ahead, cook them, cover and refrigerate them immediately. Reheat on a foil-lined baking pan for 10 to 15 minutes or until hot.

Baltimore Crab Cakes

Poached Salmon with Tarragon Cream Sauce

2 tablespoons butter or margarine
3 tablespoons minced shallot
1 clove garlic, minced
1 cup dry white wine, divided
½ cup clam juice
½ cup whipping cream
1 tablespoon chopped fresh parsley
½ teaspoon dried tarragon leaves
2 salmon steaks, 1 inch thick (about 8 ounces each)
Clam juice or water
Fresh tarragon for garnish (optional)

1. For Tarragon Cream Sauce, melt butter in medium saucepan over low heat. Add shallot and garlic; cook and stir 5 minutes or until shallot is tender. Add ½ cup wine and clam juice. Bring to a boil. Reduce heat and simmer 10 minutes or until sauce is reduced to ½ cup. Add cream; simmer 5 minutes or until sauce is reduced by half. (Sauce should heavily coat back of metal spoon.) Stir in parsley and dried tarragon; keep warm over very low heat.

2. Rinse salmon and pat dry with paper towels. Place salmon in saucepan just large enough to hold both steaks. Add remaining ½ cup wine and enough clam juice to barely cover fish. Bring wine mixture to a simmer over medium heat. (Do not boil. This will cause fish to break apart.) Adjust heat, if necessary, to keep liquid at a simmer. Simmer 10 minutes or until center is no longer red and fish flakes easily when tested with fork. Remove fish with slotted spatula; transfer to serving plates. Top fish with Tarragon Cream Sauce. Garnish, if desired. *Makes 2 servings*

Poached Salmon with Tarragon Cream Sauce

Thai Seafood Kabobs with Spicy Peanut Rice

1 ¼ cups UNCLE BEN'S® ORIGINAL CONVERTED® Brand Rice
1 pound medium raw shrimp, peeled and deveined, with tails intact
½ pound bay scallops
¼ cup soy sauce
2 tablespoons sesame oil
1 large red bell pepper, cut into 1-inch squares
6 green onions with tops, cut into 1-inch pieces
½ cup prepared Thai peanut sauce*
½ cup chopped peanuts

*Thai peanut sauce can be found in the Asian section of large supermarkets.

1. Cook rice according to package directions.

2. Meanwhile, place shrimp and scallops in medium bowl. Combine soy sauce and sesame oil; pour half of mixture over shellfish, tossing to coat. Let stand 15 minutes. Reserve remaining soy sauce mixture for basting.

3. Alternately thread shrimp, scallops, bell pepper and green onions onto twelve 12-inch metal skewers. Brush with half the reserved soy sauce mixture. Spoon Thai peanut sauce over each skewer, coating evenly. Grill or broil 8 minutes or until shrimp are pink and scallops are opaque, turning and brushing once with remaining soy sauce mixture and Thai peanut sauce.

4. Stir peanuts into cooked rice; place on serving platter. Top with seafood kabobs. Serve immediately.   *Makes 6 servings*

Serving Suggestion: Garnish with minced fresh cilantro, if desired.

Thai Seafood Kabobs with Spicy Peanut Rice

Hazelnut-Coated Salmon Steaks

¼ **cup hazelnuts**
4 **salmon steaks (about 5 ounces each)**
1 **tablespoon apple butter**
1 **tablespoon Dijon mustard**
¼ **teaspoon dried thyme leaves**
⅛ **teaspoon black pepper**
2 **cups hot cooked rice**

1. Preheat oven to 375°F. Place hazelnuts on baking sheet; bake 8 minutes or until lightly browned. Quickly transfer nuts to clean dry dish towel. Fold towel; rub vigorously to remove as much of the skins as possible. Finely chop hazelnuts using food processor.

2. Increase oven temperature to 450°F. Place salmon in single layer in baking dish. Combine apple butter, mustard, thyme and pepper in small bowl. Brush on salmon; top each steak with nuts. Bake 14 to 16 minutes or until salmon just begins to flake with fork. Serve with rice and steamed snow peas, if desired.   *Makes 4 servings*

Sole Almondine

1 **package (6.5 ounces) RICE-A-RONI® Broccoli Au Gratin**
1 **medium zucchini**
4 **sole, scrod or orange roughy fillets**
1 **tablespoon lemon juice**
¼ **cup grated Parmesan cheese, divided**
   Salt and pepper (optional)
¼ **cup sliced almonds**
2 **tablespoons margarine or butter, melted**

1. Prepare Rice-A-Roni® Mix as package directs.

2. While Rice-A-Roni® is simmering, cut zucchini lengthwise into 12 thin strips. Heat oven to 350°F.

3. In 11×7-inch glass baking dish, spread prepared rice evenly. Set aside. Sprinkle fish with lemon juice, 2 tablespoons cheese, salt and pepper, if desired. Place zucchini strips over fish; roll up. Place fish seam-side down on rice.

4. Combine almonds and margarine; sprinkle evenly over fish. Top with remaining 2 tablespoons cheese. Bake 20 to 25 minutes or until fish flakes easily with fork.

Makes 4 servings

Hazelnut-Coated Salmon Steak

Soleful Roulettes

1 package (6 ounces) long-grain and wild rice mix
1 package (3 ounces) cream cheese, softened
2 tablespoons milk
32 medium fresh spinach leaves, washed
4 sole fillets (about 1 pound)
Salt and black pepper
¼ cup dry white wine
½ cup water

1. Cook rice mix according to package directions. Place 2 cups cooked rice in large bowl. (Refrigerate remaining rice for another use.) Combine cream cheese and milk in medium bowl. Stir into rice; set aside.

2. Place spinach in heatproof bowl. Pour very hot water (not boiling) over spinach to wilt leaves slightly. Rinse sole and pat dry with paper towels. Sprinkle both sides of each fillet with salt and pepper. Cover each fillet with spinach leaves. Divide rice mixture evenly and spread over top of each spinach-lined fillet. To roll fillets, begin with thin end of fillet, roll up and secure with toothpicks.

3. Combine wine and water in large, heavy saucepan. Stand fillets upright on rolled edges in saucepan; cover. Simmer over low heat 10 minutes or until fish flakes easily when tested with fork. (Do not boil. This will cause fish to break apart.)

Makes 4 servings

Serving Suggestion: For a dinner party, serve Mediterranean Green Beans (page 225) and a salad of baby greens with oil and vinegar salad dressing. Finish the meal with a special dessert like Triple Chocolate Cake (page 302) or Premier White Lemony Cheesecake (page 290).

Soleful Roulette

Wild Rice Shrimp Paella

1½ cups canned chicken broth
2 tablespoons butter or margarine
¹⁄₁₆ teaspoon saffron *or* ⅛ teaspoon turmeric
2 boxes UNCLE BEN'S® Butter & Herb Fast Cook Recipe Long Grain & Wild Rice
1 pound medium shrimp, peeled and deveined
1 can (14½ ounces) diced tomatoes, undrained
1 cup frozen green peas, thawed
2 jars (6 ounces each) marinated artichoke hearts, drained

1. Combine broth, butter, saffron and contents of seasoning packets, reserving rice, in large saucepan. Bring to a boil.

2. Add shrimp; cook over medium-high heat 2 minutes or until shrimp turn pink. Remove shrimp with slotted spoon and set aside.

3. Add tomatoes and reserved rice. Bring to a boil. Cover; reduce heat and simmer 15 minutes.

4. Stir in peas; cover and cook 5 minutes. Add artichoke hearts and shrimp; cover and cook 5 minutes or until hot and rice is tender. Let stand 3 minutes before serving.
Makes 6 servings

Grilled Grouper

2 pounds Florida grouper fillets (or substitute snapper, shark or tilefish)
1 bottle Italian dressing
2 tablespoons lemon juice
1 teaspoon salt

Cut fish into serving size pieces and place in shallow dish. Combine Italian dressing, lemon juice and salt; pour over fish. Marinate in refrigerator 30 minutes. Brush grill with oil, then place grouper on grill over hot coals. Measure thickness of fish. Grill 10 minutes for each inch of thickness or until fish flakes when tested with fork. Turn fish halfway through cooking (unless it is less than 1 inch thick). *Makes 6 servings*

Favorite recipe from **Florida Department of Agriculture and Consumer Services, Bureau of Seafood and Aquaculture**

Wild Rice Shrimp Paella

Grilled Swordfish with Pineapple Salsa

1 tablespoon lime juice
2 cloves garlic, minced
4 swordfish steaks (5 ounces each)
½ teaspoon chili powder or black pepper
Pineapple Salsa (recipe follows)

1. Combine lime juice and garlic on plate. Dip swordfish in juice; sprinkle with chili powder.

2. Spray cold grid with nonstick cooking spray. Adjust grid 4 to 6 inches above heat. Preheat grill to medium-high heat. Grill fish, covered, 2 to 3 minutes. Turn over; grill 1 to 2 minutes more or until just opaque in center and still very moist. Top each serving with about 3 tablespoons Pineapple Salsa. *Makes 4 servings*

Pineapple Salsa

½ cup finely chopped fresh pineapple
2 cup finely chopped red bell pepper
1 green onion, thinly sliced
2 tablespoons lime juice
½ jalapeño pepper*, seeded and minced
1 tablespoon chopped fresh cilantro or fresh basil

*Jalapeño peppers can sting and irritate the skin; wear rubber gloves when handling peppers and do not touch eyes. Wash hands after handling.

Combine all ingredients in small non-metallic bowl. Serve at room temperature. Makes 1 cup salsa.

Grilled Swordfish with Pineapple Salsa

Eggplant & Shrimp over Fusilli

2 tablespoons olive oil, divided
1 large eggplant (about 1½ pounds), peeled and cut into 1-inch cubes (about 6 cups)
⅔ cup water, divided
1 medium onion, chopped
2 cloves garlic, finely chopped
¾ teaspoon salt
¼ teaspoon ground black pepper
1 jar (1 pound 10 ounces) RAGÚ® Light Pasta Sauce
8 ounces uncooked shrimp, peeled and deveined
1 box (16 ounces) fusilli pasta or spaghetti, cooked and drained
1 cup crumbled feta cheese (optional)

In 12-inch nonstick skillet, heat 1 tablespoon olive oil over medium heat and cook eggplant with ⅓ cup water, covered, stirring occasionally, 15 minutes or until eggplant is tender. Remove eggplant and set aside.

In same skillet, heat remaining 1 tablespoon olive oil over medium heat and cook onion, garlic, salt and pepper 2 minutes or until onion is tender. Stir in Ragú Light Pasta Sauce, remaining ⅓ cup water and eggplant. Reduce heat to low and simmer covered, stirring occasionally, 6 minutes. Stir in shrimp and simmer, stirring occasionally, 4 minutes or until shrimp turn pink. Serve over hot pasta and sprinkle with crumbled feta cheese, if desired.   *Makes 6 servings*

Eggplant & Shrimp over Fusilli

Vegetarian Entrées

Baked Risotto with Asparagus, Spinach & Parmesan

    1 tablespoon olive oil
    1 cup finely chopped onion
    1 cup arborio (risotto) rice
    8 cups (8 to 10 ounces) spinach leaves, torn into pieces
    2 cups chicken broth
    ¼ teaspoon salt
    ¼ teaspoon ground nutmeg
    ½ cup grated Parmesan cheese, divided
    1½ cups diagonally sliced asparagus

1. Preheat oven to 400°F. Spray 13×9-inch baking dish with nonstick cooking spray.

2. Heat olive oil in large skillet over medium-high heat. Add onion; cook and stir 4 minutes or until tender. Add rice; stir to coat with oil.

3. Stir in spinach, a handful at a time, adding more as it wilts. Add broth, salt and nutmeg. Reduce heat and simmer 7 minutes. Stir in ¼ cup cheese.

4. Transfer to prepared baking dish. Cover tightly and bake 15 minutes.

5. Remove from oven and stir in asparagus; sprinkle with remaining ¼ cup cheese. Cover and bake 15 minutes more or until liquid is absorbed.

Makes 6 entrée servings or 10 to 12 side-dish servings

Baked Risotto with Asparagus, Spinach & Parmesan

Fettuccine with Gorgonzola Sauce

8 ounces fettuccine
2 teaspoons olive oil
½ pound asparagus, cut into 1-inch pieces
1 leek, cut into ½-inch pieces
1 medium red bell pepper, cut into short strips
2 cloves garlic, minced
1 can (15 ounces) artichoke hearts, drained and quartered
1 cup cherry tomato halves
Gorgonzola Sauce (recipe follows)
¼ cup grated Parmesan cheese or crumbled Gorgonzola
Cherry tomatoes for garnish (optional)

1. Cook fettuccine according to package directions. Drain in colander. Place in large warm bowl; keep warm.

2. Meanwhile, heat oil in large skillet over medium heat. Add asparagus, leek, bell pepper and garlic; cook and stir 5 to 7 minutes or until asparagus is crisp-tender. Add artichoke hearts and tomatoes; cook 2 to 3 minutes or until hot. Add to fettuccine.

3. Prepare Gorgonzola Sauce.

4. Pour Gorgonzola Sauce over fettuccine; toss. Sprinkle with Parmesan cheese. Garnish, if desired.

Makes 4 servings

Gorgonzola Sauce

3 tablespoons butter or margarine
¼ cup all-purpose flour
2 cups milk
¼ cup vegetable broth or water
½ teaspoon black pepper
4 ounces Gorgonzola, crumbled

Melt butter in small saucepan over medium heat. Stir in flour. Cook and stir 2 to 3 minutes. Gradually stir in milk, broth and pepper. Cook until thickened, stirring constantly. Reduce heat to low. Stir in cheese until melted.

Fettuccine with Gorgonzola Sauce

Crowd-Pleasing Burritos

1 pound (2½ cups) dried pinto beans, rinsed
6 cups water
2 cups chopped onions
3 jalapeño peppers,* seeded and minced
4 cloves garlic, minced
2 teaspoons salt
16 (10-inch) flour tortillas
4 cups shredded iceberg lettuce
4 cups shredded romaine lettuce
1 cup reduced-fat sour cream
2 cups (8 ounces) shredded reduced-fat Cheddar cheese
2 cups salsa
1 cup minced fresh cilantro

*Jalapeño peppers can sting and irritate the skin; wear rubber gloves when handling peppers and do not touch eyes. Wash hands after handling peppers.

1. Place beans in Dutch oven. Cover with 2 inches of water. Bring to a boil; reduce heat to low. Simmer 5 minutes. Remove from heat and let stand, covered, 1 hour. Drain liquid from beans.

2. Add 6 cups water, onions, jalapeño peppers, garlic and salt. Bring to a boil; reduce heat to low. Simmer, covered, 1 hour or until beans are tender. Drain cooking broth from beans.

3. Preheat oven to 300°F. Stack tortillas and wrap in foil. Bake 20 minutes or until heated through.

4. Combine lettuces. Top tortillas with beans, lettuces, sour cream, cheese, salsa and cilantro. Fold in 2 sides; roll to enclose filling.   *Makes 16 servings*

Crowd-Pleasing Burrito

Spinach Phyllo Bundle

1 tablespoon vegetable oil
¼ cup finely chopped onion
1 package (10 ounces) frozen chopped spinach, thawed and
    squeezed dry
1 package (10 ounces) frozen artichoke hearts, thawed and cut into
    quarters
1 cup small broccoli florets, steamed
2 red bell peppers, seeded, cut into squares and roasted
1 cup (4 ounces) shredded Monterey Jack cheese
¾ cup grated Parmesan cheese
1 cup minced fresh cilantro
¼ teaspoon ground nutmeg
6 to 8 tablespoons butter or margarine, melted
12 sheets frozen phyllo dough, thawed
    Fresh cilantro for garnish

1. Heat oil in large skillet over medium heat until hot. Cook and stir onion 3 minutes. Add spinach; cook 5 minutes or until spinach is dry.

2. Add artichoke hearts, broccoli and bell peppers to skillet; cook and stir 2 to 3 minutes or until heated through. Remove from heat; stir in cheeses, cilantro and nutmeg.

3. Preheat oven to 375°F. Brush 12-inch pizza pan with butter. Unroll phyllo dough. Cover with plastic wrap and damp, clean kitchen towel to prevent phyllo from drying out.

4. Lay one sheet phyllo dough on clean surface; brush top with butter. Fold crosswise in half and place on pizza pan. Brush with butter.

5. Repeat with remaining phyllo dough sheets and butter, arranging phyllo in pinwheel fashion on pan.

6. Spoon spinach mixture onto phyllo, making a mound 8 inches in diameter. Bring up several phyllo dough sheets at a time over filling; repeat with remaining phyllo dough. Brush with butter.

7. Bake 40 to 45 minutes or until golden brown. Let stand 5 to 10 minutes; cut into wedges.

Makes 6 to 8 servings

Spinach Phyllo Bundle

Pesto Lasagna

1 package (16 ounces) uncooked lasagna noodles
3 tablespoons olive oil
1½ cups chopped onions
3 cloves garlic, finely chopped
3 packages (10 ounces each) frozen chopped spinach, thawed and squeezed dry
Salt
Black pepper
3 cups (24 ounces) ricotta cheese
1½ cups prepared pesto sauce
¾ cup grated Parmesan cheese
½ cup pine nuts, toasted
6 cups (16 ounces) shredded mozzarella cheese
Strips of roasted red pepper (optional)

1. Preheat oven to 350°F. Oil 13×9-inch casserole or lasagna pan. Partially cook lasagna noodles according to package directions.

2. Heat oil in large skillet. Cook and stir onions and garlic until transparent. Add spinach; cook and stir about 5 minutes. Season with salt and pepper. Transfer to large bowl.

3. Add ricotta cheese, pesto, Parmesan cheese and pine nuts to spinach mixture; mix well.

4. Layer 5 lasagna noodles, slightly overlapping, in prepared casserole. Top with ⅓ of ricotta mixture and ⅓ of mozzarella. Repeat layers twice.

5. Bake about 35 minutes or until hot and bubbly. Garnish with red bell pepper, if desired.

Makes 8 servings

Pesto Lasagna

Grilled Panini Sandwiches

8 slices country Italian, sourdough or other firm-textured bread
8 slices SARGENTO® Deli Style Sliced Mozzarella Cheese
⅓ cup prepared pesto
4 large slices ripe tomato
2 tablespoons olive oil

1. Top each of 4 slices of bread with a slice of cheese. Spread pesto over cheese. Arrange tomatoes on top, then another slice of cheese. Close sandwiches with remaining 4 slices bread.

2. Brush olive oil lightly over both sides of sandwiches. Cook sandwiches over medium-low coals or in a preheated ridged grill pan over medium heat 3 to 4 minutes per side or until bread is toasted and cheese is melted. *Makes 4 servings*

Speedy Garden Roll-Ups

1 cup hummus
1 tablespoon finely chopped cilantro
4 (6-inch) flour tortillas
½ cup shredded carrot
½ cup shredded red cabbage
½ cup (2 ounces) shredded reduced-fat Cheddar cheese
4 red leaf lettuce leaves

1. Combine hummus and cilantro.

2. Spread each tortilla with ¼ cup hummus mixture to about ½ inch from edge. Sprinkle evenly with 2 tablespoons each carrot, cabbage and cheese. Top with 1 lettuce leaf.

3. Roll up tortillas jelly-roll fashion. Seal with additional hummus mixture.

4. Serve immediately or wrap tightly with plastic wrap and refrigerate up to 4 hours. *Makes 4 servings*

Grilled Panini Sandwich

Rice, Cheese & Bean Enchiladas

1 (2-cup) bag UNCLE BEN'S® Boil-in-Bag Rice
4 cups shredded zucchini, drained (2 medium)
1 tablespoon reduced-sodium taco sauce mix
1 can (15 ounces) pinto beans, rinsed and drained
1 can (10 ounces) reduced-fat, reduced-sodium cream of
mushroom soup
1 can (8 ounces) diced green chilies
12 (8-inch) flour tortillas
2 cups (8 ounces) reduced-fat Mexican cheese blend, divided

1. Prepare rice following package directions.

2. Combine zucchini and taco sauce mix in large nonstick skillet. Cook and stir zucchini 5 minutes. Add beans, soup, chilies and rice. Bring to a boil.

3. Spray 13×9-inch microwavable baking dish with nonstick cooking spray. Spoon about ½ cup of rice mixture onto center of each tortilla. Top with 2 tablespoons cheese. Roll up to enclose filling; place in baking dish. Sprinkle remaining cheese over enchiladas. Microwave at HIGH 4 minutes or until cheese is melted.

Makes 6 servings

Serving Suggestion: Serve with sliced mango or orange sections.

Rice, Cheese & Bean Enchilada

Cheddar and Leek Strata

8 eggs, lightly beaten
2 cups milk
½ cup ale or beer
2 cloves garlic, minced
¼ teaspoon salt
¼ teaspoon black pepper
1 loaf (16 ounces) sourdough bread, cut into ½-inch cubes
2 small leeks, coarsely chopped
1 red bell pepper, chopped
1½ cups (6 ounces) shredded Swiss cheese
1½ cups (6 ounces) shredded sharp Cheddar cheese
Fresh sage sprigs for garnish (optional)

1. Combine eggs, milk, ale, garlic, salt and black pepper in large bowl. Beat until well blended.

2. Place ½ of bread cubes on bottom of greased 13×9-inch baking dish. Sprinkle ½ of leeks and ½ of bell pepper over bread cubes. Top with ¾ cup Swiss cheese and ¾ cup Cheddar cheese. Repeat layers with remaining ingredients, ending with Cheddar cheese.

3. Pour egg mixture evenly over top. Cover tightly with plastic wrap or foil. Weigh top of strata down with slightly smaller baking dish. Refrigerate strata at least 2 hours or overnight.

4. Preheat oven to 350°F. Bake, uncovered, 40 to 45 minutes or until center is set. Garnish with fresh sage, if desired. Serve immediately. *Makes 12 servings*

Cheddar and Leek Strata

Lasagna Florentine

2 tablespoons olive oil
3 medium carrots, finely chopped
1 package (8 to 10 ounces) sliced mushrooms
1 medium onion, finely chopped
2 cloves garlic, finely chopped
1 jar (1 pound 10 ounces) RAGÚ® Robusto! Pasta Sauce
1 container (15 ounces) ricotta cheese
2 cups shredded mozzarella cheese, divided
1 box (10 ounces) frozen chopped spinach, thawed and squeezed dry
¼ cup grated Parmesan cheese
2 eggs
1 teaspoon salt
1 teaspoon dried Italian seasoning
16 lasagna noodles, cooked and drained

Preheat oven to 375°F. In 12-inch skillet, heat olive oil over medium heat and cook carrots, mushrooms, onion and garlic until carrots are almost tender, about 5 minutes. Stir in Pasta Sauce; heat through.

Meanwhile, in medium bowl, combine ricotta cheese, 1½ cups mozzarella cheese, spinach, Parmesan cheese, eggs, salt and Italian seasoning; set aside.

In 13×9-inch baking dish, evenly spread ½ cup sauce mixture. Arrange 4 lasagna noodles, lengthwise over sauce, overlapping edges slightly. Spread ⅓ of the ricotta mixture over noodles; repeat layers, ending with noodles. Top with remaining sauce and ½ cup mozzarella cheese. Cover with foil and bake 40 minutes. Remove foil and continue baking 10 minutes or until bubbling. *Makes 8 servings*

Lasagna Florentine

Bean Ragoût with Cilantro-Cornmeal Dumplings

2 cans (14½ ounces each) diced tomatoes, undrained
1 can (15½ ounces) pinto or kidney beans, rinsed and drained
1 can (15½ ounces) black beans, rinsed and drained
1½ cups chopped red bell pepper
1 large onion, chopped
2 small zucchini, sliced
½ cup chopped green bell pepper
½ cup chopped celery
1 poblano chili pepper,* seeded and chopped
2 cloves garlic, minced
3 tablespoons chili powder
2 teaspoons ground cumin
1 teaspoon dried oregano leaves
¼ teaspoon salt
⅛ teaspoon black pepper
Cilantro-Cornmeal Dumplings (recipe follows)

Chili peppers can sting and irritate the skin; wear rubber gloves when handling peppers and do not touch eyes.

Slow Cooker Directions

1. Combine tomatoes with juice, beans, red bell pepper, onion, zucchini, green bell pepper, celery, poblano pepper, garlic, chili powder, cumin, oregano, ¼ teaspoon salt and black pepper in slow cooker; mix well. Cover; cook on LOW 7 to 8 hours.

2. Prepare dumplings 1 hour before serving. *Turn slow cooker to HIGH.* Drop dumplings by level tablespoonfuls (larger dumplings will not cook properly) on top of ragoût. Cover; cook 1 hour or until toothpick inserted into dumpling comes out clean.

Makes 6 servings

Cilantro-Cornmeal Dumplings: Combine ¼ cup all-purpose flour, ¼ cup cornmeal, ½ teaspoon baking powder and ¼ teaspoon salt in medium bowl. Cut in 1 tablespoon shortening with pastry blender until mixture resembles coarse crumbs. Stir in 1 tablespoon shredded Cheddar cheese and 2 teaspoons minced fresh cilantro. Stir in ¼ cup milk, stirring until just blended.

Classic Fettuccine Alfredo

¾ **pound uncooked fettuccine**
 6 tablespoons unsalted butter
⅔ **cup heavy or whipping cream**
½ **teaspoon salt**
   Generous dash white pepper
   Generous dash ground nutmeg
 1 cup freshly grated Parmesan cheese (about 3 ounces)
 2 tablespoons chopped fresh parsley
   Fresh Italian parsley sprig for garnish

1. Cook fettuccine in large pot of boiling salted water 6 to 8 minutes or just until al dente; remove from heat. Drain well; return to pot.

2. Place butter and cream in large, heavy skillet over medium-low heat. Cook and stir until butter melts and mixture bubbles. Cook and stir 2 minutes more. Stir in salt, pepper and nutmeg. Remove from heat. Gradually stir in cheese until well blended and smooth. Return briefly to heat to completely blend cheese if necessary. (Do not let sauce bubble or cheese will become lumpy and tough.)

3. Pour sauce over fettuccine. Stir and toss with 2 forks over low heat 2 to 3 minutes until sauce is thickened and fettuccine is evenly coated. Sprinkle with chopped parsley. Garnish, if desired. Serve immediately.   *Makes 4 servings*

Cabbage-Cheese Strudel

1 tablespoon vegetable oil
1 cup chopped onions
½ cup sliced leeks
½ cup sliced button mushrooms
½ cup seeded and chopped tomato
¼ head green cabbage, shredded
1 cup broccoli florets, steamed
1½ teaspoons caraway seeds, crushed, divided
1 teaspoon dried dill weed
½ teaspoon salt
¼ teaspoon black pepper
1 package (8 ounces) cream cheese, softened
¾ cup cooked brown rice
¾ cup (3 ounces) shredded Cheddar cheese
1 egg, beaten
6 sheets frozen phyllo pastry, thawed
6 to 8 tablespoons margarine or butter, melted

1. Heat oil in large saucepan over medium heat until hot. Add onions and leeks; cook and stir 3 minutes. Add mushrooms and tomato; cook and stir 5 minutes. Add cabbage, broccoli, 1 teaspoon caraway seeds, dill weed, salt and pepper. Cover; cook over medium heat 8 to 10 minutes or until cabbage wilts. Remove cover; cook 10 minutes more or until cabbage is soft and beginning to brown.

2. Combine cream cheese, rice, Cheddar cheese and egg in medium bowl. Stir into cabbage mixture until blended.

3. Preheat oven to 375°F. Unroll phyllo dough. Cover with plastic wrap and damp, clean kitchen towel. Brush 1 phyllo dough sheet with margarine. Top with 2 more sheets, brushing each with margarine. Spoon half of cabbage mixture 2 inches from short end of phyllo. Spread mixture to cover about half of phyllo. Roll up dough from short end with filling. Place, seam side down, on greased cookie sheet. Flatten roll slightly with hands and brush with margarine. Repeat with remaining phyllo, margarine and cabbage mixture. Sprinkle tops of rolls with remaining ½ teaspoon caraway seeds.

4. Bake 45 to 50 minutes or until golden brown. Cool 10 minutes. Cut each roll diagonally into 3 pieces with serrated knife. *Makes 6 servings*

Cabbage-Cheese Strudel

soups & salads

California Crab Salad

1 packet (.4 ounce) HIDDEN VALLEY® The Original Ranch® Buttermilk Recipe Salad Dressing Mix
1 cup buttermilk
1 cup mayonnaise
1 tablespoon grated fresh ginger
1 teaspoon prepared horseradish
2 cups cooked white rice, chilled
4 lettuce leaves
8 ounces cooked crabmeat, chilled
1 large ripe avocado, thinly sliced
½ medium cucumber, thinly sliced

In medium bowl, whisk together salad dressing mix, buttermilk and mayonnaise. Whisk in ginger and horseradish. Cover and refrigerate 30 minutes. To serve, arrange ½ cup rice on top of each lettuce leaf. Top with 2 tablespoons of the dressing. Arrange one quarter of the crabmeat, avocado and cucumber on top of each rice mound. Serve with remaining dressing. Garnish with cherry tomatoes and lime wedges, if desired. *Makes 4 servings*

Serving Suggestion: For a delicious lunch, serve with Zucchini-Orange Bread (page 272) or Cherry Orange Poppy Seed Muffins (page 272). Finish off the meal with a dessert of Tempting Chocolate Mousse (page 296).

California Crab Salad

Sausage and Chicken Gumbo

1 tablespoon canola oil
1 red bell pepper, chopped
1 pound boneless skinless chicken thighs, trimmed of excess fat and cut into 1-inch pieces
1 package (12 ounces) chicken sausage in Cajun andouille or chili flavor, sliced ½ inch thick
½ cup chicken broth
1 can (28 ounces) crushed tomatoes with roasted garlic
¼ cup finely chopped green onions
1 bay leaf
½ teaspoon dried basil leaves
½ teaspoon black pepper
¼ to ½ teaspoon red pepper flakes
6 lemon wedges (optional)

1. Heat oil in large saucepan. Add bell pepper; cook and stir over medium-high heat 2 to 3 minutes. Add chicken; cook and stir about 2 minutes or until browned. Add sausage; cook and stir 2 minutes or until browned. Add chicken broth; scrape up any browned bits from bottom of saucepan.

2. Add tomatoes, green onions, bay leaf, basil, black pepper and red pepper flakes. Simmer 15 minutes. Remove and discard bay leaf. Garnish each serving with lemon wedge, if desired. *Makes 6 servings*

Serving Suggestion: Serve this gumbo with Herb-Cheese Biscuit Loaf (page 258) or your favorite corn bread.

Sausage and Chicken Gumbo

Layered Southwest Salad

        Creamy Ranch-Style Dressing (recipe follows)
    1 jicama (¾ pound), peeled and cut into 8 wedges
    1 can (15 ounces) black beans, drained and rinsed
    ⅔ cup salsa
    ½ cup diced red onion
    10 ounces spinach, washed, stemmed and chopped
        1 package (10 ounces) frozen corn, cooked, drained and cooled
        4 large hard-cooked eggs, peeled and sliced
    1½ cups (6 ounces) shredded Cheddar cheese
        Fresh oregano for garnish

Prepare Creamy Ranch-Style Dressing. Cut jicama wedges crosswise into ⅛-inch-thick slices. Combine beans, salsa and onion in medium bowl. Layer half of spinach, jicama, bean mixture, corn, eggs and Creamy Ranch-Style Dressing in large salad bowl. Repeat first 5 layers beginning with spinach and ending with eggs; sprinkle with cheese. Drizzle with remaining dressing. Cover and refrigerate 1 to 2 hours before serving. Garnish, if desired.   *Makes 6 servings*

Creamy Ranch-Style Dressing

    ⅔ cup cottage cheese
    ½ cup buttermilk
    1 tablespoon white wine vinegar
    1 large clove garlic
    ½ teaspoon salt
    ½ teaspoon ground cumin
    ½ teaspoon dried oregano leaves
    ½ teaspoon black pepper

Combine all ingredients in blender; cover and process until smooth. Cover and refrigerate 1 hour.   *Makes 1¼ cups dressing*

Layered Southwest Salad

Sausage & Rice Soup

2 tablespoons butter or margarine
1 large or 2 medium leeks, white and light green parts sliced
2 carrots, thinly sliced
1 package (16 ounces) JENNIE-O TURKEY STORE® Extra Lean
    Smoked Sausage
2 cans (13¾ ounces each) reduced-sodium chicken broth
2 cups diced mixed bell peppers, preferably red and yellow
1 cup water
¾ cup quick-cooking brown rice, uncooked
½ teaspoon dried sage
¼ teaspoon freshly ground black pepper
    Chopped fresh chives (optional)

Melt butter in large saucepan over medium heat. Add leeks and carrots; cook 5 minutes, stirring occasionally. Meanwhile, cut sausage into ½-inch slices; remove and discard casings, if desired. Add sausage to saucepan; cook 5 minutes, stirring occasionally. Add broth, bell peppers, water, rice, sage and pepper; bring to a boil over high heat. Reduce heat; simmer uncovered 15 minutes or until sausage is no longer pink in center and rice is tender. Ladle into bowls; top with chives, if desired.

Makes 6 servings

Serving Suggestion: Serve with Cheddar and Apple Muffins (page 254) and ice cream sundaes for dessert.

Smoky Pasta Salad with Jack Cheese

4 pieces bacon, cut into ¼-inch strips
¾ cup *French's*® *Gourmayo*™ Smoked Chipotle Light Mayonnaise
½ cup milk or water
2 cups (6 ounces) uncooked thin spaghetti, broken into thirds
1½ cups pear or cherry tomatoes (cut in half if large)
1 cup cubed Monterey Jack cheese with jalapeño (½-inch cubes)
½ cup chopped Italian parsley
Romaine lettuce leaves

1. Cook bacon in saucepan until crisp. Remove with slotted spoon; reserve. Stir mayonnaise and milk into pan with drippings. Heat through; set aside.

2. Cook pasta according to package directions using shortest cooking time; drain. Transfer to bowl. Add tomatoes, cheese and parsley.

3. Pour dressing over all and toss. Serve over lettuce leaves. Sprinkle with reserved cooked bacon. *Makes 4 servings*

Tip: Reheat pasta salad in microwave before serving, if desired.

Prep Time: 10 minutes
Cook Time: 10 minutes

Mediterranean Shrimp and Feta Spring Salad

1 pound large raw shrimp in the shell
1 teaspoon salt
4 cups (6 ounces) baby spinach
2 large plum tomatoes, cored and chopped
¼ cup chopped green onions, green and white parts
¼ cup coarsely chopped pitted kalamata olives
2 ounces feta cheese, crumbled
1 tablespoon minced fresh oregano or basil
3 tablespoons extra-virgin olive oil
1 tablespoon red wine vinegar
1 tablespoon small capers
½ teaspoon freshly ground black pepper

1. Place shrimp in large saucepan with 1 quart of water. Add salt; bring to simmer over medium-high heat. Simmer 8 to 10 minutes or until shrimp are firm and white. Drain and set aside until cool enough to handle. Peel and cut into bite-size pieces.

2. Place shrimp in large salad bowl. Add spinach, tomatoes, green onions, olives, feta and oregano. Combine olive oil, vinegar, capers and pepper in a small bowl. Stir well. Pour over salad and toss gently.   *Makes 4 servings*

Cranky Crab Bisque

¾ pound lump crabmeat *or* 2 (6-ounce) cans crabmeat
⅓ cup dry sherry
1 (11-ounce) can tomato soup, undiluted
1 (11-ounce) can green pea soup, undiluted
1 teaspoon TABASCO® brand Pepper Sauce
2 cups milk

Combine crabmeat and sherry in medium bowl; marinate 15 minutes. Heat soups and TABASCO® Sauce in 3-quart saucepan over low heat. Stir in milk until well blended and mixture is heated through. Just before serving, stir in crabmeat mixture; cook until heated through.   *Makes 6 servings*

Mediterranean Shrimp and Feta Spring Salad

Chicken and Wild Rice Soup

3 cans (14½ ounces each) chicken broth
1 pound boneless skinless chicken breasts or thighs, cut into
   bite-size pieces
2 cups water
1 cup sliced celery
1 cup diced carrots
1 package (6 ounces) converted long grain and wild rice mix with
   seasoning packet (not quick-cooking or instant rice)
½ cup chopped onion
½ teaspoon black pepper
 2 teaspoons white vinegar (optional)
 1 tablespoon dried parsley flakes

Slow Cooker Directions

1. Combine broth, chicken, water, celery, carrots, rice and seasoning packet, onion and pepper in slow cooker; mix well.

2. Cover; cook on LOW 6 to 7 hours or on HIGH 4 to 5 hours or until chicken is tender.

3. Stir in vinegar, if desired. Sprinkle with parsley.   *Makes 9 (1½-cup) servings*

Prep Time: 20 minutes
Cook Time: 6 to 7 hours

Serving Suggestion: Serve with warm crusty bread for a light lunch or with a grilled cheese, bacon and tomato sandwich.

Chicken and Wild Rice Soup

Famous Crab Rice Salad

1 bag SUCCESS® Rice
1 package (6 ounces) frozen crabmeat, thawed
1 cup sliced celery
¾ cup chopped seeded tomato
½ cup chopped onion
¼ cup reduced-calorie mayonnaise
2 tablespoons cider vinegar
1 tablespoon olive oil
1 tablespoon hot pepper sauce
1 tablespoon Dijon mustard
1 clove garlic, minced
½ teaspoon salt
½ teaspoon dried basil leaves, crushed

Prepare rice according to package directions. Cool.

Place rice in large bowl. Add crabmeat, celery, tomato, onion and mayonnaise; mix lightly. Combine vinegar, oil, hot pepper sauce, mustard, garlic, salt and basil in jar with tight-fitting lid; shake well. Pour over rice mixture; toss gently to coat. Refrigerate 2 hours. Garnish, if desired. *Makes 6 to 8 servings*

Serving Suggestion: Serve with Lemon Poppy Seed Muffins (page 268) and cinnamon butter.

Famous Crab Rice Salad

Potato & Spinach Soup with Gouda

9 medium Yukon Gold potatoes, peeled and cubed (about 6 cups)
2 cans (14 ounces each) chicken broth
½ cup water
1 small red onion, finely chopped
5 ounces baby spinach leaves
½ teaspoon salt
¼ teaspoon ground red pepper
¼ teaspoon black pepper
2½ cups shredded smoked Gouda cheese, divided
1 can (12 ounces) evaporated milk
1 tablespoon olive oil
4 cloves garlic, cut into thin slices
5 to 7 sprigs parsley, finely chopped

Slow Cooker Directions

1. Combine potatoes, chicken broth, water, red onion, spinach, salt, red and black pepper in slow cooker.

2. Cover; cook on LOW 10 hours or until potatoes are tender.

3. Slightly mash potatoes in slow cooker; add 2 cups Gouda and evaporated milk. Cover; cook on HIGH 15 to 20 minutes or until cheese is melted.

4. Heat oil in small skillet over low heat. Cook and stir garlic until golden brown; set aside. Pour soup into bowls. Sprinkle 2 to 3 teaspoons remaining Gouda cheese in each bowl. Add spoonful of garlic to center of each bowl; sprinkle with parsley.

Makes 8 to 10 servings

Potato & Spinach Soup with Gouda

Near East Steak Salad

⅔ cup *French's*® Honey Dijon Mustard
½ cup water
¼ cup teriyaki sauce
2 tablespoons grated peeled ginger
1 teaspoon minced garlic
1 pound boneless sirloin or flank steak (1 inch thick)
8 cups mixed salad greens, washed and torn
1 medium yellow or orange bell pepper, thinly sliced
2 green onions, thinly shredded
¼ cup chopped dry roasted peanuts

1. Combine mustard, water, teriyaki sauce, ginger and garlic in small bowl. Pour 1 cup dressing into small serving bowl.

2. Broil or grill steak 10 minutes or until desired doneness, basting with remaining ½ cup dressing. Let stand 5 minutes.

3. Thinly slice steak. Serve over salad greens. Top with bell pepper, green onions and peanuts. Drizzle with reserved dressing.

Makes 4 servings

Prep Time: 10 minutes
Cook Time: 10 minutes

tip

To easily remove the skin from fresh ginger, use the edge of a spoon to scrape away the thin skin.

Near East Steak Salad

Mediterranean Lentil Soup

2 tablespoons olive oil
1 large onion, diced
1 stalk celery, chopped
2 large cloves garlic, finely minced
1 can (28 ounces) peeled whole plum tomatoes, drained and chopped
1½ cups dried lentils, soaked in cold water 1 hour, drained and rinsed*
1 tablespoon tomato paste
1½ teaspoons dried thyme leaves
6 cups beef broth
2 bay leaves

Vinaigrette
¾ cup packed fresh basil leaves
⅓ cup olive oil
2 tablespoons minced fresh parsley
2 tablespoons red wine vinegar
Salt and black pepper

Add 1 to 2 hours to cooking time if lentils are not soaked.

Slow Cooker Directions

1. Heat 2 tablespoons oil in large saucepan over medium heat. Add onion, celery and garlic; cook and stir 5 minutes. Stir in tomatoes, lentils, tomato paste and thyme. Combine lentil mixture, broth and bay leaves in slow cooker; mix well.

2. Cover; cook on LOW 8 hours or on HIGH 4 hours or until lentils are soft.

3. Meanwhile, prepare vinaigrette. Combine basil, ⅓ cup oil, parsley and vinegar in blender or food processor. Blend until smooth. Stir vinaigrette into soup just before serving. Season with salt and pepper. *Makes 4 to 6 servings*

Variation: Alternatively, place all soup ingredients except vinaigrette in slow cooker. Stir to combine; cover; cook on LOW 8 hours or on HIGH 4 hours.

Salmon, Asparagus & Orzo Salad

1 (8-ounce) salmon fillet
1 cup uncooked orzo pasta
8 ounces asparagus spears, cut into 2-inch lengths (about 1½ cups), cooked
½ cup dried cranberries
¼ cup sliced green onions
3 tablespoons extra-virgin olive oil
1 tablespoon white wine vinegar
1½ teaspoons Dijon mustard
½ teaspoon salt
⅛ teaspoon black pepper

1. Prepare grill for direct grilling. Grill salmon on oiled grid over medium coals about 10 minutes per inch of thickness or until opaque. Remove from grill; cool. Flake salmon into bite-size pieces.

2. Meanwhile, cook orzo according to package directions, omitting salt; drain and cool.

3. Combine salmon, orzo, asparagus, cranberries and green onions in large bowl. Whisk together olive oil, vinegar, mustard, salt and pepper until well blended. Pour over salmon mixture; toss until coated. Chill 30 minutes to 1 hour.

Makes 4 to 6 servings

Tip: The salmon fillet may be cooked a day ahead; cover and refrigerate until you're ready to make the salad.

sandwiches & wraps

Asian Wraps

>   **Nonstick cooking spray**
>   **8 ounces boneless skinless chicken breasts or thighs, cut into ½-inch pieces**
>   **1 teaspoon minced fresh ginger**
>   **1 teaspoon minced fresh garlic**
>   **¼ teaspoon red pepper flakes**
>   **¼ cup reduced-sodium teriyaki sauce**
>   **4 cups (about 8 ounces) packaged coleslaw mix**
>   **½ cup sliced green onions**
>   **4 (10-inch) flour tortillas**
>   **8 teaspoons no-sugar-added plum fruit spread**

1. Spray nonstick wok or large skillet with cooking spray; heat over medium-high heat. Stir-fry chicken 2 minutes. Add ginger, garlic and pepper flakes; stir-fry 2 minutes. Add teriyaki sauce; mix well.* Add coleslaw mix and green onions; stir-fry 4 minutes or until chicken is no longer pink and cabbage is crisp-tender.

2. Spread each tortilla with 2 teaspoons fruit spread; evenly spoon chicken mixture down center of tortillas. Roll up to form wraps. *Makes 4 servings*

*If sauce is too thick, add up to 2 tablespoons water to thin it.

Prep Time: 10 minutes
Cook Time: 10 minutes

Asian Wraps

Jamaican Chicken Sandwiches

1 teaspoon Jerk Seasoning (recipe follows)
4 boneless skinless chicken breasts (about 1 pound)
2 tablespoons reduced-fat mayonnaise
2 tablespoons plain nonfat yogurt
1 tablespoon mango chutney
4 onion rolls (2 ounces each), split and toasted
4 lettuce leaves
8 slices peeled mango or papaya

1. Prepare Jerk Seasoning. Sprinkle chicken with Jerk Seasoning and set aside. Spray grid with nonstick cooking spray. Prepare grill for direct cooking.

2. Place chicken on grid, 3 to 4 inches from medium-hot coals. Grill 5 to 7 minutes on each side or until no longer pink in center.

3. Combine mayonnaise, yogurt and chutney in small bowl; spread 1 tablespoonful onto each onion roll.

4. Place chicken on onion roll bottoms; top each with lettuce leaf, 2 slices of mango and roll top. *Makes 4 servings*

Prep Time: 8 minutes
Cook Time: 14 minutes

Jerk Seasoning

1½ teaspoons salt
1½ teaspoons ground allspice
1 teaspoon sugar
1 teaspoon dried ground thyme leaves
1 teaspoon black pepper
½ teaspoon garlic powder
½ teaspoon ground red pepper
¼ teaspoon ground cinnamon
¼ teaspoon ground nutmeg

Combine all ingredients in small bowl. Store in tightly covered jar.

Jamaican Chicken Sandwich

Grilled Steak & Blue Cheese Sandwiches

6 to 8 cloves Grilled Garlic (recipe follows), mashed
4 boneless lean, tender beef steaks, such as beef tenderloin or top loin steaks (4 to 6 ounces each), 1 inch thick
Freshly ground or cracked black pepper
2 medium yellow onions
Olive oil
4 French rolls
½ cup crumbled blue cheese
2 small tomatoes, sliced
Mixed greens

Prepare Grilled Garlic. Spread garlic onto both sides of steaks; season generously with pepper. Slice onions into ½-inch-thick slices; brush lightly with oil. Insert wooden picks into onion slices from edges to prevent separating into rings. (Soak wooden picks in hot water 15 minutes to prevent burning.) Lightly oil grid to prevent sticking. Place steaks in center of covered grill over medium-hot KINGSFORD® Briquets; place onion slices around steaks. Grill steaks and onion slices 12 to 15 minutes or until steaks are medium-rare or to desired doneness, turning once. Remove steaks from grill; keep warm. Move onions to center of grill and continue grilling 10 to 15 minutes longer until tender and golden brown. Grill rolls, cut sides down, until toasted. Slice steaks into thin strips. Arrange beef over grilled rolls; top with blue cheese, onions, tomatoes and greens. *Makes 4 sandwiches*

Grilled Garlic

1 or 2 heads garlic
Olive oil

Peel outermost papery skin from garlic heads. Brush heads with oil. Grill heads at edge of grid on covered grill over medium-hot KINGSFORD® Briquets 30 to 45 minutes or until cloves are soft and buttery. Remove from grill; cool slightly. Gently squeeze softened garlic head from root end so that cloves slip out of skins into small bowl. Use immediately or cover and refrigerate up to 1 week.

Grilled Steak & Blue Cheese Sandwiches

Ranch Burgers

1¼ pounds lean ground beef
¾ cup prepared HIDDEN VALLEY® The Original Ranch® Dressing
¾ cup dry bread crumbs
¼ cup minced onion
1 teaspoon salt
¼ teaspoon black pepper
Sesame seed buns
Lettuce, tomato slices and red onion slices (optional)
Additional HIDDEN VALLEY® The Original Ranch® Dressing

In large bowl, combine beef, salad dressing, bread crumbs, onion, salt and pepper. Shape into 6 patties. Grill over medium-hot coals 5 to 6 minutes until no longer pink in center (160°F). Place on sesame seed buns with lettuce, tomato and red onion slices, if desired. Serve with a generous amount of additional salad dressing.

Makes 6 servings

Grilled Eggplant Sandwiches

1 eggplant (about 1¼ pounds)
Salt and black pepper
6 thin slices provolone cheese
6 thin slices deli-style ham or mortadella
Fresh basil leaves (optional)
Olive oil

Cut eggplant into 12 (⅜-inch-thick) rounds; sprinkle both sides with salt and pepper. Top each of 6 eggplant slices with slice of cheese, slice of ham (fold or tear to fit) and a few basil leaves, if desired. Cover with slice of eggplant. Brush one side with olive oil. Secure each sandwich with 2 or 3 toothpicks.

Oil hot grid to help prevent sticking. Grill eggplant, oil side down, on covered grill, over medium KINGSFORD® Briquets, 15 to 20 minutes. Halfway through cooking time, brush top with oil, then turn and continue grilling until eggplant is tender when pierced. (When turning, position sandwiches so toothpicks extend down between spaces in grid.) If eggplant starts to char, move to cooler part of grill. Let sandwiches cool about 5 minutes, then cut into halves or quarters, if desired. Serve warm or at room temperature.

Makes 6 sandwiches

Ranch Burger

Chili Beef & Red Pepper Fajitas with Chipotle Salsa

6 ounces boneless beef top sirloin steak, thinly sliced
½ lime
1½ teaspoons chili powder
½ teaspoon ground cumin
½ cup diced plum tomatoes
¼ cup mild picante sauce
½ canned chipotle pepper in adobo sauce
** Nonstick cooking spray**
½ cup sliced onion
½ red bell pepper, cut into thin strips
2 (10-inch) fat-free flour tortillas, warmed
¼ cup fat-free sour cream
2 tablespoons chopped fresh cilantro leaves (optional)

1. Place steak on plate. Squeeze lime juice over steak; sprinkle with chili powder and cumin. Coat well; let stand 10 minutes.

2. Meanwhile, to prepare salsa, combine tomatoes and picante sauce in small bowl. Place chipotle on small plate. Using fork, mash completely. Stir mashed chipotle into tomato mixture.

3. Coat 12-inch skillet with cooking spray. Heat over high heat until hot. Add onion and bell pepper; cook and stir 3 minutes or until edges begin to blacken. Remove from skillet. Lightly spray skillet with cooking spray. Add beef; stir-fry 1 minute. Return onion and bell pepper to skillet; cook 1 minute longer.

4. Place ½ the beef mixture in center of each tortilla; fold sides over filling. Top each fajita with ¼ cup salsa, 2 tablespoons sour cream and cilantro, if desired.

Makes 2 servings

Note: For a less spicy salsa, use less chipotle chili or eliminate it completely.

Chili Beef & Red Pepper Fajita with Chipotle Salsa

Caramelized Onion, Brie & Smoked Ham Croissants

¼ cup I CAN'T BELIEVE IT'S NOT BUTTER!® Spread
1 large Spanish onion, thinly sliced
8 slices Canadian bacon (about 4 ounces)
4 large heated croissants, halved lengthwise, or bagels, split and toasted
8 ounces Brie cheese, cut into ⅛-inch wedges

Preheat oven to 350°F.

In 12-inch skillet, melt I Can't Believe It's Not Butter!® Spread over medium-high heat and cook onion, stirring occasionally, 10 minutes or until golden brown. Remove onion and set aside.

In same skillet, heat bacon, turning once.

On baking sheet, arrange 4 croissant halves. Evenly top with bacon, then onions, then cheese. Bake 2 minutes or until cheese is slightly melted. Top with remaining croissant halves and serve hot.   *Makes 4 servings*

Best Ever Beef Heroes

3 tablespoons mayonnaise
1 tablespoon Dijon mustard
2 teaspoons prepared horseradish
4 submarine or hoagie rolls, split
4 red leaf or romaine lettuce leaves
1 pound sliced deli roast beef
1 thin slice red onion, separated into rings
8 slices SARGENTO® Deli Style Sliced Swiss Cheese

1. Combine mayonnaise, mustard and horseradish; mix well. Spread on cut sides of rolls.

2. Fill rolls with lettuce, roast beef, onion rings and cheese. Close sandwiches; cut in half.   *Makes 4 servings*

Preparation Time: 10 minutes

Caramelized Onion, Brie & Smoked Ham Croissants

Shredded BBQ Chicken Sandwiches

1 jar (26 ounces) RAGÚ® Old World Style® Pasta Sauce
3 tablespoons firmly packed brown sugar
2 tablespoons apple cider vinegar
1½ tablespoons chili powder
2 teaspoons garlic powder
1½ teaspoons onion powder
4 boneless, skinless chicken breast halves (about 1¼ pounds)
6 hamburger buns or round rolls

1. In 6-quart saucepot, cook Ragú Pasta Sauce, brown sugar, vinegar, chili powder, garlic powder and onion powder over medium heat, stirring occasionally, 5 minutes.

2. Season chicken, if desired, with salt and ground black pepper. Add chicken to sauce. Reduce heat to medium-low and simmer covered, stirring occasionally, 20 minutes or until chicken is no longer pink in center. Remove saucepot from heat.

3. Remove chicken from sauce. Using two forks, shred chicken. Return shredded chicken to sauce and heat through. To serve, arrange chicken mixture on buns and garnish, if desired, with shredded Cheddar cheese.   *Makes 6 servings*

Prep Time: 5 minutes
Cook Time: 30 minutes

Georgia Grilled Ham & Cheese Sandwiches

⅓ cup peach preserves
¼ cup mayonnaise or salad dressing
1½ cups shredded Monterey Jack cheese
2 (5-ounce) cans HORMEL® chunk ham, drained and flaked
¼ cup toasted, chopped pecans
8 slices firm white bread
2 tablespoons melted butter

In small bowl, combine peach preserves and mayonnaise. Add cheese, ham and chopped pecans; stir to combine. Divide ham mixture evenly among 4 bread slices. Top with remaining bread. Brush outside of each sandwich with melted butter. Place sandwich on hot griddle or in large nonstick skillet. Cook over medium heat, until filling is hot and bread is lightly browned on both sides, turning once.   *Makes 6 servings*

Shredded BBQ Chicken Sandwich

Open-Faced Italian Focaccia Sandwiches

2 cups shredded cooked chicken
½ cup HIDDEN VALLEY® The Original Ranch® Dressing
¼ cup diagonally sliced green onions
1 piece focaccia bread, about ¾-inch thick, 10×7-inches
2 medium tomatoes, thinly sliced
4 cheese slices, such as provolone, Cheddar or Swiss
2 tablespoons grated Parmesan cheese (optional)

Stir together chicken, dressing and onions in a small mixing bowl. Arrange chicken mixture evenly on top of focaccia. Top with layer of tomatoes and cheese slices. Sprinkle with Parmesan cheese, if desired. Broil 2 minutes or until cheese is melted and bubbly.   *Makes 4 servings*

Note: Purchase rotisserie chicken at your favorite store to add great taste and save preparation time.

Souper Stuffed Cheese Burgers

1 envelope LIPTON® RECIPE SECRETS® Onion Soup Mix*
2 pounds ground beef
½ cup water
¾ cup shredded Cheddar, mozzarella or Monterey Jack cheese
** (about 6 ounces)**

*Also terrific with LIPTON® RECIPE SECRETS® Savory Herb with Garlic, Onion Mushroom or Beefy Onion Soup Mix.

1. In large bowl, combine soup mix, ground beef and water; shape into 12 patties.

2. Place 2 tablespoons cheese in center of 6 patties. Top with remaining patties and seal edges tightly.

3. Grill or broil until burgers are done (160°F). Serve, if desired, on onion poppy seed rolls.   *Makes 6 servings*

Tip: To perk up your burgers, serve them on something besides a bun. Try bagels, English muffins, pita bread or even tortillas for a fun change of pace!

Open-Faced Italian Focaccia Sandwich

Mu Shu Turkey Wraps

1 can (16 ounces) plums, drained and pitted
½ cup orange juice
¼ cup finely chopped onion
1 tablespoon minced fresh ginger
¼ teaspoon ground cinnamon
1 pound boneless turkey breast, cut into thin strips
6 (7-inch) flour tortillas
3 cups coleslaw mix

Slow Cooker Directions

1. Place plums in blender or food processor. Cover and blend until almost smooth. Combine plums, orange juice, onion, ginger and cinnamon in slow cooker; mix well.

2. Place turkey over plum mixture. Cover; cook on LOW 3 to 4 hours.

3. Remove turkey from slow cooker. Divide evenly among tortillas. Spoon about 2 tablespoons plum sauce over turkey in each tortilla; top with about ½ cup coleslaw mix. Fold bottom edge of tortilla over filling; fold in sides. Roll up to completely enclose filling. Repeat with remaining tortillas. Use remaining plum sauce for dipping.

Makes 6 servings

Serving Suggestion: Serve with a light first course of won ton or egg drop soup from your local Chinese restaurant. A dessert of Tempting Chocolate Mousse (page 296) or Sautéed Mangoes & Peaches with Peanut Brittle Topping (page 278) completes the meal.

Mu Shu Turkey Wrap

Italian Combo Subs

1 tablespoon vegetable oil
1 pound boneless beef round steak, cut into thin strips
1 pound bulk Italian sausage
1 green bell pepper, cut into strips
1 medium onion, thinly sliced
1 can (4 ounces) sliced mushrooms, drained (optional)
   Salt
   Black pepper
1 jar (26 ounces) spaghetti sauce
2 loaves French bread, cut into 6-inch pieces and split

Slow Cooker Directions

1. Heat oil in large skillet over medium-high heat. Brown beef strips in two batches. Place beef in slow cooker.

2. In same skillet, brown sausage, stirring to separate meat. Drain and discard fat. Add sausage to slow cooker.

3. Place bell pepper, onion and mushrooms, if desired, over meat in slow cooker. Season with salt and black pepper. Top with spaghetti sauce. Cover; cook on LOW 4 to 6 hours. Serve in bread rolls. *Makes 6 servings*

Serving Suggestion: Top with freshly grated Parmesan cheese.

Italian Combo Sub

side dishes

Mediterranean Vegetable Bake

2 tomatoes, sliced
1 small red onion, sliced
1 medium zucchini, sliced
1 small eggplant, sliced
1 large portobello mushroom, sliced
2 cloves garlic, finely chopped
3 tablespoons olive oil
2 teaspoons chopped fresh rosemary
⅔ cup dry white wine
    Salt
    Black pepper

1. Preheat oven to 350°F. Oil bottom of oval casserole or 13×9-inch baking dish.

2. Arrange slices of vegetables in rows, alternating different types and overlapping slices in casserole to make attractive arrangement. Sprinkle garlic evenly over top. Mix olive oil with rosemary in small bowl; spread over top.

3. Pour wine over vegetables; season with salt and pepper. Loosely cover with foil. Bake 20 minutes. Uncover and bake an additional 10 to 15 minutes or until vegetables are soft.   *Makes 4 to 6 servings*

Mediterranean Vegetable Bake

Spicy Beans Tex-Mex

⅓ **cup lentils**
1⅓ **cups water**
5 **strips bacon**
1 **onion, chopped**
1 **can (15 ounces) pinto beans, rinsed and drained**
1 **can (15 ounces) red kidney beans, rinsed and drained**
1 **can (14½ ounces) diced tomatoes, undrained**
3 **tablespoons ketchup**
3 **cloves garlic, minced**
1 **teaspoon chili powder**
½ **teaspoon ground cumin**
¼ **teaspoon red pepper flakes**
1 **bay leaf**

Slow Cooker Directions

1. Boil lentils in water 20 to 30 minutes in large saucepan; drain. Cook bacon in medium skillet until crisp. Remove to paper towels. Crumble bacon. In same skillet, cook onion in bacon drippings until soft.

2. Combine lentils, bacon, onion, beans, tomatoes with juice, ketchup, garlic, chili powder, cumin, pepper flakes and bay leaf in slow cooker.

3. Cover; cook on LOW 5 to 6 hours or on HIGH 3 to 4 hours. Remove bay leaf before serving. *Makes 8 to 10 servings*

Prep Time: 35 minutes
Cook Time: 5 to 6 hours

Spicy Beans Tex-Mex

Broccoli Casserole with Crumb Topping

2 slices day-old white bread, coarsely crumbled (about 1¼ cups)
½ cup shredded mozzarella cheese (about 2 ounces)
2 tablespoons chopped fresh parsley (optional)
2 tablespoons BERTOLLI® Olive Oil, divided
1 clove garlic, finely chopped
6 cups broccoli florets and/or cauliflowerets
1 envelope LIPTON® RECIPE SECRETS® Onion Soup Mix
1 cup water
1 large tomato, chopped

1. In small bowl, combine bread crumbs, cheese, parsley, if desired, 1 tablespoon oil and garlic; set aside.

2. In 12-inch skillet, heat remaining 1 tablespoon oil over medium heat and cook broccoli, stirring frequently, 2 minutes.

3. Stir in onion soup mix blended with water. Bring to a boil over high heat. Reduce heat to low and simmer uncovered, stirring occasionally, 8 minutes or until broccoli is almost tender. Add tomato and simmer 2 minutes.

4. Spoon vegetable mixture into 1½-quart casserole; top with bread crumb mixture. Broil 1½ minutes or until crumbs are golden and cheese is melted.

Makes 6 servings

Carrots Amandine

1 pound carrots, peeled and cut into ½-inch diagonal slices
¼ cup golden raisins (optional)
¼ cup I CAN'T BELIEVE IT'S NOT BUTTER!® Spread
3 tablespoons honey
1 teaspoon lemon juice
¼ teaspoon ground ginger (optional)
¼ cup sliced almonds, toasted

On stovetop or in microwave oven, steam carrots and raisins, if desired, until carrots are tender; drain. Stir in I Can't Believe It's Not Butter!® Spread, honey, lemon juice and ginger, if desired. Spoon into serving bowl and sprinkle with almonds.

Makes 4 servings

Note: Recipe can be halved.

Broccoli Casserole with Crumb Topping

Cabbage Wedges with Tangy Hot Dressing

1 slice bacon, cut crosswise into ¼-inch strips
2 teaspoons cornstarch
⅔ cup unsweetened apple juice
¼ cup cider or red wine vinegar
1 tablespoon brown sugar
½ teaspoon caraway seeds
1 green onion, thinly sliced
½ head red or green cabbage (about 1 pound), cut into 4 wedges

1. Cook bacon in large skillet over medium heat until crisp. Remove bacon with slotted spoon to paper towel; set aside. Meanwhile, dissolve cornstarch in apple juice in small bowl. Stir in vinegar, brown sugar and caraway seeds; set aside. Add onion to hot drippings in skillet. Cook and stir until onion is soft but not brown.

2. Place cabbage wedges, flat side down, in skillet. Add cornstarch mixture to skillet. Cook over medium heat 4 minutes. Carefully turn over cabbage wedges. Cook 6 minutes or until cabbage is fork-tender and dressing is thickened.

3. Remove cabbage to cutting board; carefully cut away core. Transfer to warm serving plates. Pour hot dressing over cabbage wedges. Sprinkle with bacon pieces. Garnish as desired. Serve immediately. *Makes 4 servings*

Grilled Corn In The Husk

6 ears corn (with husks)
⅓ cup butter, melted
1 tablespoon LAWRY'S® Seasoned Salt
1 teaspoon LAWRY'S® Seasoned Pepper

Peel husks back carefully and remove silk. In small glass bowl, combine butter, Seasoned Salt and Seasoned Pepper. Brush each ear of corn with seasoned butter. Smooth husks over corn and tie ends together with kitchen string. Grill corn on medium heat for 20 minutes, turning every 5 minutes. *Makes 6 servings*

Variation: For a fat-free variation, cook corn without seasoned butter. Instead, squeeze fresh lime juice over corn; sprinkle with Seasoned Salt and Seasoned Pepper.

Prep Time: 13 minutes
Cook Time: 20 minutes

Cabbage Wedges with Tangy Hot Dressing

Spinach and Mushroom Risotto

Nonstick olive oil cooking spray
½ pound mushrooms, sliced
2 teaspoons dried basil leaves
2 teaspoons minced garlic
¼ teaspoon black pepper
1 can (about 14 ounces) chicken broth
1½ cups uncooked arborio rice
1 can (10¾ ounces) condensed cream of mushroom soup, undiluted
1⅔ cups water
3 cups packed spinach leaves, chopped
6 tablespoons chopped walnuts, toasted
¼ cup grated Parmesan cheese

1. Spray 3-quart saucepan with cooking spray; heat over high heat. Add mushrooms, basil, garlic and pepper; cook and stir 3 to 4 minutes or until mushrooms are tender.

2. Stir in broth, rice, soup and water; cook and stir until well blended and mixture begins to boil. Reduce heat to low. Cover; simmer gently 14 minutes, stirring twice during cooking or until rice is just tender but still firm to the bite.

3. Stir in spinach; cover and let stand 5 to 7 minutes or until spinach is wilted.

4. Sprinkle with walnuts and cheese before serving.   *Makes 8 servings*

tip

Arborio rice is traditionally used for risotto because its high starch content produces a creamy dish. This recipe may be served as a main dish if you wish—it makes 4 to 5 servings.

Spinach and Mushroom Risotto

Swiss-Style Vegetables

1 unpeeled red potato, cubed
2 cups broccoli florets
1 cup cauliflower florets
2 teaspoons margarine
1 cup sliced mushrooms
1 tablespoon all-purpose flour
1 cup milk
½ cup (2 ounces) reduced-fat shredded Swiss cheese
¼ teaspoon salt
¼ teaspoon black pepper
¼ teaspoon hot pepper sauce (optional)
⅛ teaspoon ground nutmeg
¼ cup grated Parmesan cheese

1. Place potato in medium saucepan; cover with cold water. Bring water to a boil. Reduce heat; cover and simmer 10 minutes. Add broccoli and cauliflower; cover and cook about 5 minutes or until all vegetables are tender. Drain; remove vegetables and set aside.

2. Melt margarine in same pan over medium-low heat. Add mushrooms. Cook and stir 2 minutes. Stir in flour; cook 1 minute. Slowly stir in milk; cook and stir until mixture thickens. Remove from heat. Add Swiss cheese, stirring until melted. Stir in salt, pepper, hot sauce, if desired, and nutmeg.

3. Preheat broiler. Spray small shallow casserole with nonstick cooking spray.

4. Arrange vegetables in single layer in prepared casserole. Spoon sauce mixture over vegetables; sprinkle with Parmesan cheese.

5. Place casserole under broiler until cheese melts and browns, about 1 minute.

Makes 6 (½-cup) servings

Vegetable Couscous

3 cups water
1 package KNORR® Recipe Classics™ Vegetable Soup, Dip and Recipe Mix
2 tablespoons BERTOLLI® Olive Oil or I CAN'T BELIEVE IT'S NOT BUTTER!® Spread
1 package (10 ounces) plain couscous (about 1½ cups)
¼ cup chopped fresh parsley (optional)
Pine nuts, slivered almonds or raisins (optional)

● In 2-quart saucepan, bring water, recipe mix and olive oil to a boil, stirring frequently. Reduce heat; cover and simmer 2 minutes.

● Stir couscous into saucepan until evenly moistened. Remove from heat; cover and let stand 5 minutes.

● Fluff couscous with fork. Spoon into serving dish. Garnish, if desired, with chopped parsley and nuts or raisins. *Makes 5 cups couscous*

Tip: Turn Vegetable Couscous into an easy one-dish meal. Just add 2 cups cut-up cooked chicken or turkey to the saucepan in step 1.

Prep Time: 5 minutes
Cook Time: 10 minutes

Vegetables & Wild Rice

1 box UNCLE BEN'S® Long Grain & Wild Rice Roasted Garlic
2⅓ cups water
2 tablespoons butter or margarine
1 cup corn, fresh or frozen
1 medium tomato, chopped
4 strips bacon, cooked and crumbled
3 tablespoons chopped green onions

COOK: CLEAN: Wash hands. In medium skillet, combine water, butter, rice and contents of seasoning packet. Bring to a boil. Cover tightly and simmer 15 minutes. Add corn and simmer 15 minutes or until water is absorbed. Stir in tomato and bacon. Sprinkle with green onions.

SERVE: Serve with garlic toast, if desired.

CHILL: Refrigerate leftovers immediately.   *Makes 6 servings*

Cheesy Potato Gratin

3½ pounds baking potatoes, peeled and thinly sliced
2 tablespoons HERB-OX® chicken flavored bouillon granules, divided
3 cups shredded Havarti cheese, divided
6 tablespoons all-purpose flour, divided
3 cups heavy whipping cream

Heat oven to 400°F. Spray a 13×9-inch baking dish with nonstick cooking spray. Arrange ⅓ of the potatoes in the dish. Sprinkle with 1 teaspoon bouillon and season to taste with freshly ground pepper. Add ⅓ of the cheese and 2 tablespoons flour. Continue adding two more layers of potatoes, bouillon, pepper, flour and cheese. In bowl, combine whipping cream and remaining 1 tablespoon chicken bouillon. Pour mixture over the potatoes. Bake for 60 minutes or until the top is golden brown and the potatoes are tender.   *Makes 10 to 12 servings*

Prep Time: 20 minutes
Total Time: 1 hour, 20 minutes

Vegetables & Wild Rice

Sautéed Snow Peas & Baby Carrots

**1 tablespoon I CAN'T BELIEVE IT'S NOT BUTTER!® Spread
2 tablespoons chopped shallots or onion
5 ounces frozen whole baby carrots, partially thawed
4 ounces snow peas (about 1 cup)
2 teaspoons chopped fresh parsley (optional)**

In 12-inch nonstick skillet, melt I Can't Believe It's Not Butter!® Spread over medium heat and cook shallots, stirring occasionally, 1 minute or until almost tender. Add carrots and snow peas and cook, stirring occasionally, 4 minutes or until crisp-tender. Stir in parsley, if desired, and heat through.   *Makes 2 servings*

Note: Recipe can be doubled.

Original Green Bean Casserole

**1 can (10¾ ounces) condensed cream of mushroom soup
¾ cup milk
⅛ teaspoon ground black pepper
2 packages (9 ounces each) frozen cut green beans, thawed*
1⅓ cups *French's*® French Fried Onions, divided**

**Substitute 2 cans (14½ ounces each) cut green beans, drained, for frozen green beans.*

1. Preheat oven to 350°F. Combine soup, milk and pepper in 1½-quart casserole; stir until well blended. Stir in beans and ⅔ cup French Fried Onions.

2. Bake, uncovered, 30 minutes or until hot; stir. Sprinkle with remaining ⅔ *cup* onions. Bake 5 minutes or until onions are golden brown.   *Makes 6 servings*

Microwave Directions: Prepare green bean mixture as above; pour into 1½-quart microwave-safe casserole. Cover with vented plastic wrap. Microwave on HIGH 8 to 10 minutes or until heated through, stirring halfway through cooking time. Uncover. Top with remaining onions. Cook 1 minute until onions are golden. Let stand 5 minutes.

Substitution: You can substitute 4 cups cooked cut fresh green beans for the frozen or canned.

Prep Time: 5 minutes
Cook Time: 35 minutes

Sautéed Snow Peas & Baby Carrots

Spanish Paella-Style Rice

2 cans (14½ ounces each) chicken broth
1½ cups uncooked converted long grain rice
1 small red bell pepper, diced
⅓ cup dry white wine or water
½ teaspoon powdered saffron or turmeric
⅛ teaspoon red pepper flakes
½ cup frozen peas, thawed
Salt

Slow Cooker Directions

1. Combine broth, rice, bell pepper, wine, saffron and pepper flakes in slow cooker; mix well.

2. Cover; cook on LOW 4 hours or until liquid is absorbed.

3. Stir in peas. Cover; cook on LOW 15 to 30 minutes or until peas are hot. Season with salt.   *Makes 6 servings*

Variations: Add ½ cup cooked chicken, ham or shrimp or quartered marinated artichokes, drained, with peas.

Note: Paella is a Spanish dish of saffron-flavored rice combined with a variety of meats, seafood and vegetables. Paella is traditionally served in a wide, shallow dish. Since saffron is expensive, turmeric is given as an alternative; with turmeric the dish will look similar but the flavor will differ.

Prep Time: 10 minutes
Cook Time: 4½ hours

Spanish Paella-Style Rice

Orange-Spiced Sweet Potatoes

2 pounds sweet potatoes, peeled and diced
½ cup packed dark brown sugar
½ cup butter (1 stick), cut in small pieces
 Juice of 1 medium orange
1 teaspoon ground cinnamon
1 teaspoon vanilla
½ teaspoon ground nutmeg
½ teaspoon grated orange peel
¼ teaspoon salt
 Chopped toasted pecans (optional)

Slow Cooker Directions

Place all ingredients in slow cooker, except pecans. Cover and cook on LOW 4 hours or on HIGH 2 hours or until potatoes are tender. Sprinkle with pecans before serving, if desired. *Makes 8 (½-cup) servings*

Variation: Mash potatoes with a hand masher or electric mixer; add ¼ cup milk or cream for a moister consistency. Sprinkle with a mixture of sugar and cinnamon.

Brussels Sprouts and Carrots with Honey Mustard Butter

1 pound Brussels sprouts
½ pound baby carrots
3 tablespoons butter
2 tablespoons honey mustard
½ teaspoon salt
 Black pepper, to taste

1. Trim Brussels sprouts; cut in half (or quarters if large). Combine brussels sprouts and carrots in medium saucepan; cover with cold water. Bring to a boil over high heat. Reduce heat; simmer 8 minutes or until tender. Drain.

2. Melt butter in same saucepan over medium heat; stir in mustard, salt and pepper. Return vegetables to saucepan; toss to coat with sauce. *Makes 8 servings*

Tip: Vegetables may be prepared up to 2 hours before serving and transferred to a microwavable casserole. Reheat in microwave oven just before serving.

Orange-Spiced Sweet Potatoes

Orzo with Spinach and Red Pepper

4 ounces uncooked orzo
Nonstick cooking spray
1 teaspoon olive oil
1 medium red bell pepper, diced
3 cloves garlic, minced
1 package (10 ounces) frozen chopped spinach, thawed and
squeezed dry
¼ cup grated Parmesan cheese
½ teaspoon minced fresh oregano or basil leaves (optional)
¼ teaspoon lemon pepper

1. Prepare orzo according to package directions; drain well and set aside.

2. Spray large nonstick skillet with cooking spray. Heat skillet over medium-high heat until hot; add oil, tilting skillet to coat bottom. Add bell pepper and garlic; cook and stir 2 to 3 minutes or until bell pepper is crisp-tender. Add orzo and spinach; stir until well mixed and heated through. Remove from heat and stir in Parmesan cheese, oregano, if desired, and lemon pepper. Garnish as desired. *Makes 6 servings*

Grilled Summer Vegetables Alouette®

1 large aluminum foil cooking bag
3 cups fresh broccoli florets
3 cups sliced summer squash (any type)
2 medium red bell peppers, cut into strips
1 cup sliced mushrooms
1 (6.5-ounce) package or two (4-ounce) packages ALOUETTE®
Garlic & Herbs

Preheat grill to medium high. Open foil bag, layer vegetables evenly inside, and spoon Alouette cheese on top. Seal bag by double-folding end. Place on grill and cook 8 to 10 minutes. Using oven mitts, carefully place bag on baking sheet and cut open, allowing steam to escape. If bag sticks to grill rack, cut open and remove vegetables (after grill cools, peel off bag). *Makes 6 servings*

For oven cooking: Preheat oven to 450°F. Insert ingredients as above. Bake sealed bag on baking sheet 20 to 25 minutes.

Orzo with Spinach and Red Pepper

Southwestern Rice

1 cup uncooked converted rice
1 can (15 ounces) black beans, rinsed and drained
1 can (8 ounces) corn, drained
1 packet (1 ounce) HIDDEN VALLEY® The Original Ranch® Salad
Dressing & Seasoning Mix
¾ cup (3 ounces) diced Monterey Jack cheese
½ cup diced seeded tomato
¼ cup sliced green onions

Cook rice according to package directions, omitting salt. During last 5 minutes of cooking time, quickly uncover and add beans and corn; cover immediately. When rice is done, remove saucepan from heat; stir in salad dressing & seasoning mix. Let stand 5 minutes. Stir in cheese, tomato and onions. Serve immediately.

Makes 6 servings

Roast Herbed Sweet Potatoes with Bacon & Onions

3 thick slices applewood-smoked bacon or peppered bacon, diced
2 pounds sweet potatoes, peeled and cut into 2-inch chunks
2 medium onions, cut into 8 wedges
1 teaspoon dried thyme leaves
1 teaspoon salt
¼ teaspoon black pepper

1. Preheat oven to 375°F. Cook bacon in large, deep skillet until crisp. Remove from heat. Drain bacon on paper towels; set aside. Add potatoes and onions to skillet; toss with drippings. Add thyme, salt and pepper; toss again.

2. Spread mixture in single layer in 15×10-inch jelly-roll pan or shallow roasting pan. Bake 40 to 50 minutes or until golden brown and tender. Transfer to serving bowl; top with bacon.

Makes 10 to 12 servings

Tip: Potatoes can be prepared and baked up to 2 hours before serving; let them stand at room temperature. Reheat the sweet potatoes at 375°F for 20 minutes.

Mediterranean Green Beans

1 pound fresh green beans, cut into 1½-inch pieces
12 small cherry tomatoes
¼ cup chopped red onion
½ cup grated BELGIOIOSO® Asiago
⅓ cup chopped parsley
2 tablespoons water
2 tablespoons white wine vinegar
1 tablespoon olive oil
1 clove garlic, minced
¼ teaspoon dried thyme
¼ teaspoon black pepper

Steam beans, covered, 8 minutes or until crisp-tender. Drain beans; plunge into cold water and drain again. Combine beans, tomatoes and onion in medium bowl.

Combine cheese and remaining ingredients in small bowl, stirring until well blended. Pour over vegetables, tossing gently to coat. Serve at room temperature.

Makes 12 servings

tip

This colorful dish is an excellent choice to serve with Apple Stuffed Pork Loin Roast (page 88), Chicken Tuscany (page 90), Soleful Roulettes (page 132) or Classic Fettuccine Alfredo (page 159).

brunch dishes

Individual Spinach & Bacon Quiches

   3 slices bacon
   ½ small onion, diced
   1 package (9 ounces) frozen chopped spinach, thawed, drained and squeezed dry
   ½ teaspoon black pepper
   ⅛ teaspoon ground nutmeg
   Pinch salt
   1 container (15 ounces) whole milk ricotta cheese
   2 cups (8 ounces) shredded mozzarella cheese
   1 cup grated Parmesan cheese
   3 eggs, lightly beaten

1. Preheat oven to 350°F. Spray 10 muffin pan cups with nonstick cooking spray.

2. Cook bacon in large skillet over medium-high heat until crisp. Drain; cool and crumble.

3. In same skillet, cook and stir onion in remaining bacon fat 5 minutes or until tender. Add spinach, pepper, nutmeg and salt. Cook and stir over medium heat about 3 minutes or until liquid evaporates. Remove from heat. Stir in bacon; cool.

4. Combine ricotta, mozzarella and Parmesan cheeses in large bowl. Add eggs; stir until well blended. Add cooled spinach mixture; mix well.

5. Divide mixture evenly among prepared muffin cups. Bake 40 minutes or until filling is set. Let stand 10 minutes. Run thin knife around edges to release. Serve hot or refrigerate and serve cold.   *Makes 10 servings*

Individual Spinach & Bacon Quiches

Orange Coffeecake with Streusel Topping

1 package (about 19 ounces) cinnamon swirl muffin mix
1 egg
1 teaspoon grated orange peel
¾ cup orange juice
½ cup pecan pieces
½ cup powdered sugar (optional)
1 tablespoon milk (optional)

1. Preheat oven to 400°F. Grease 9-inch square baking pan; set aside.

2. Place muffin mix in large bowl; break up any lumps. Add egg, orange peel and juice; stir until just moistened. (Batter will be slightly lumpy.)

3. Knead cinnamon swirl packet 10 seconds. Cut off 1 end of packet; squeeze contents over batter. Swirl into batter using knife or spatula. Do not mix in completely.

4. Spoon batter into prepared pan; sprinkle with topping packet and pecans. Bake 23 to 25 minutes or until toothpick inserted into center of cake comes out almost clean. Cool in pan on wire rack 15 minutes.

5. To prepare icing, if desired, combine powdered sugar and milk in small bowl; stir until smooth. Drizzle icing over top of cooled coffeecake.   *Makes 9 servings*

Orange Coffeecake with Streusel Topping

Spinach Sensation

½ **pound bacon slices**
1 **cup (8 ounces) sour cream**
3 **eggs, separated**
2 **tablespoons all-purpose flour**
⅛ **teaspoon black pepper**
1 **package (10 ounces) frozen chopped spinach, thawed and
    squeezed dry**
½ **cup (2 ounces) shredded sharp Cheddar cheese**
½ **cup dry bread crumbs**
1 **tablespoon margarine or butter, melted**

1. Preheat oven to 350°F. Spray 2-quart round baking dish with nonstick cooking spray.

2. Place bacon in single layer in large skillet; cook over medium heat until crisp. Remove from skillet; drain on paper towels. Crumble and set aside.

3. Combine sour cream, egg yolks, flour and pepper in large bowl; set aside. Beat egg whites in medium bowl at high speed of electric mixer until stiff peaks form. Stir ¼ of egg whites into sour cream mixture; fold in remaining egg whites.

4. Arrange half of spinach in prepared dish. Top with half of sour cream mixture. Sprinkle ¼ cup cheese over sour cream mixture. Sprinkle bacon over cheese. Repeat layers, ending with remaining ¼ cup cheese.

5. Combine bread crumbs and margarine in small bowl; sprinkle evenly over cheese. Bake, uncovered, 30 to 35 minutes or until egg mixture is set. Let stand 5 minutes before serving. *Makes 6 servings*

tip

Spinach Sensation may be served for brunch with fresh fruit, for lunch with sliced tomatoes or as a light dinner with a green salad or a fruit salad.

Spinach Sensation

Hash Brown Casserole

6 eggs, well beaten
1 can (12 fluid ounces) NESTLÉ® CARNATION® Evaporated Milk
1 teaspoon salt
½ teaspoon ground black pepper
1 package (30 ounces) frozen shredded hash brown potatoes
2 cups (8 ounces) shredded cheddar cheese
1 medium onion, chopped
1 small green bell pepper, chopped
1 cup diced ham (optional)

PREHEAT oven to 350°F. Grease 13×9-inch baking dish.

COMBINE eggs, evaporated milk, salt and black pepper in large bowl. Add potatoes, cheese, onion, bell pepper and ham, if desired; mix well. Pour mixture into prepared baking dish.

BAKE for 60 to 65 minutes or until set. *Makes 12 servings*

Note: For a lower-fat version of this recipe, use 3 cartons (4 ounces *each*) cholesterol-free egg product, substitute NESTLÉ® CARNATION® Evaporated Fat Free Milk for Evaporated Milk and 10 slices turkey bacon, cooked and chopped, for the diced ham. Proceed as above.

Hash Brown Casserole

Gooey Caramel and Chocolate Pecan Rolls

2 loaves (1 pound each) frozen white bread dough
1 jar (12 ounces) caramel ice cream topping
⅔ cup coarsely chopped pecans
1 cup semisweet chocolate chips, divided
4 tablespoons butter, divided

1. Thaw bread dough according to package directions.

2. Preheat oven to 375°F. Divide caramel topping evenly between two 9-inch round cake pans; spread in thin layers. Sprinkle pecans evenly over caramel.

3. Microwave ⅔ cup chocolate chips and 2 tablespoons butter in medium microwavable bowl at HIGH (100% power) 30 seconds; stir. Microwave at 20-second intervals, if necessary, stirring until smooth; set aside.

4. On lightly floured surface, roll 1 loaf bread dough into 12×8-inch rectangle. Spread half chocolate mixture over dough. Beginning from long side, roll up, jelly-roll style, to form 12-inch log, pinching seam to seal. Slice into 12 rolls; arrange cut sides down in one prepared pan. Repeat with remaining dough, chocolate mixture and second pan.

5. Cover; let rise in warm place until nearly doubled, about 1 hour. Uncover; bake 20 to 25 minutes. Immediately invert onto serving plates.

6. Melt remaining ⅓ cup chocolate chips and 2 tablespoons butter in microwave as directed in step 3. Drizzle over warm rolls.   *Makes 24 rolls*

Gooey Caramel and Chocolate Pecan Rolls

Cheddar Broccoli Quiche

1½ **cups milk**
3 **eggs**
1 **package KNORR® Recipe Classics™ Leek Soup, Dip and Recipe Mix**
1 **package (10 ounces) frozen chopped broccoli, thawed and drained**
1½ **cups shredded Cheddar, Swiss or Monterey Jack cheese**
    (about 6 ounces)
1 **(9-inch) unbaked or frozen deep-dish pie crust***

If using 9-inch deep-dish frozen prepared pie crust, do not thaw. Preheat oven and cookie sheet. Pour filling into pie crust; bake on cookie sheet.

● Preheat oven to 375°F. In large bowl, with fork, beat milk, eggs and recipe mix until blended. Stir in broccoli and cheese; spoon into pie crust.

● Bake 40 minutes or until knife inserted 1 inch from edge comes out clean. Let stand 10 minutes before serving.   *Makes 6 servings*

Tip: Cheddar Broccoli Quiche, accompanied with fresh fruit or cherry tomatoes, is perfect for brunch or lunch. Or, serve it with a mixed green salad and soup for a hearty dinner.

Prep Time: 10 minutes
Cook Time: 40 minutes

Cheddar Broccoli Quiche

Banana Bread Waffles with Cinnamon Butter

½ cup unsalted whipped butter, softened
2 tablespoons powdered sugar
2 teaspoons grated orange peel
¼ teaspoon ground cinnamon
¼ teaspoon vanilla
1 package (7 ounces) banana muffin mix
⅔ cup buttermilk
1 egg

1. Preheat waffle iron.

2. Combine butter, powdered sugar, orange peel, cinnamon and vanilla in small bowl; mix well. Set aside. Combine muffin mix, buttermilk and egg in medium bowl; stir until just blended.

3. Spray waffle iron with nonstick cooking spray. Spoon 1 cup batter into waffle iron; cook according to manufacturer's directions. Repeat with remaining batter. Spoon butter mixture onto each waffle. *Makes 4 servings*

Brunch Sausage Casserole

4 cups cubed day-old bread
2 cups (8 ounces) shredded sharp cheddar cheese
2 cans (12 fluid ounces *each*) NESTLÉ® CARNATION® Evaporated Milk
10 eggs, lightly beaten
1 teaspoon dry mustard
¼ teaspoon onion powder
   Ground black pepper to taste
1 package (16 ounces) fresh breakfast sausage, cooked, drained and crumbled

GREASE 13×9-inch baking dish. Place bread in prepared dish. Sprinkle with cheese. Combine evaporated milk, eggs, dry mustard, onion powder and pepper in medium bowl. Pour over bread mixture. Sprinkle with sausage. Cover; refrigerate overnight.

PREHEAT oven to 325°F.

BAKE for 55 to 60 minutes or until cheese is golden brown. Cover with foil if top browns too quickly. *Makes 10 to 12 servings*

Banana Bread Waffles with Cinnamon Butter

Chili Cheese Puff

¾ cup all-purpose flour
1½ teaspoons baking powder
9 eggs
4 cups (16 ounces) shredded Monterey Jack cheese
2 cups (16 ounces) 1% low-fat cottage cheese
2 cans (4 ounces each) diced green chilies, drained
1½ teaspoons sugar
¼ teaspoon salt
⅛ teaspoon hot pepper sauce
1 cup prepared salsa

1. Preheat oven to 350°F. Spray 13×9-inch baking dish with nonstick cooking spray.

2. Combine flour and baking powder in small bowl.

3. Whisk eggs in large bowl until blended; stir in Monterey Jack, cottage cheese, chilies, sugar, salt and hot pepper sauce. Add flour mixture; stir just until combined. Pour into prepared dish.

4. Bake, uncovered, 45 minutes or until set. Let stand 5 minutes before serving. Serve with salsa.

Makes 8 servings

Chili Cheese Puff

French Toast Strata

4 ounces day-old French or Italian bread, cut into ¾-inch cubes (4 cups)
⅓ cup golden raisins
1 package (3 ounces) cream cheese, cut into ¼-inch cubes
3 eggs
1½ cups milk
½ cup maple-flavored pancake syrup
1 teaspoon vanilla
2 tablespoons sugar
1 teaspoon ground cinnamon
Additional maple-flavored pancake syrup (optional)

1. Spray 11×7-inch baking dish with nonstick cooking spray. Place bread cubes in even layer in prepared dish; sprinkle raisins and cream cheese evenly over bread.

2. Beat eggs in medium bowl with electric mixer at medium speed until blended. Add milk, ½ cup pancake syrup and vanilla; mix well. Pour egg mixture evenly over bread mixture. Cover; refrigerate at least 4 hours or overnight.

3. Preheat oven to 350°F. Combine sugar and cinnamon in small bowl; sprinkle evenly over strata.

4. Bake, uncovered, 40 to 45 minutes or until puffed, golden brown and knife inserted into center comes out clean. Cut into squares and serve with additional pancake syrup, if desired.

Makes 6 servings

Serving Suggestion: Serve with fresh fruit compote.

French Toast Strata

Cranberry Orange Ring

2 cups all-purpose flour
1 cup sugar
1 ½ teaspoons baking powder
1 teaspoon salt
½ teaspoon baking soda
¼ teaspoon ground cloves
1 tablespoon grated orange peel
¾ cup orange juice
1 egg, lightly beaten
2 tablespoons vegetable oil
1 teaspoon vanilla
¼ teaspoon orange extract
1 cup whole cranberries

1. Preheat oven to 350°F. Grease 12-cup tube pan; set aside.

2. Combine flour, sugar, baking powder, salt, baking soda and cloves in large bowl. Add orange peel; mix well. Set aside. Combine orange juice, egg, oil, vanilla and orange extract in medium bowl. Beat until well blended. Add orange juice mixture to flour mixture. Stir until just moistened. Gently fold in cranberries. Do not overmix.

3. Spread batter evenly in prepared pan. Bake 30 to 35 minutes (35 to 40 minutes if using frozen cranberries) or until toothpick inserted near center comes out clean. Cool in pan on wire rack 15 to 20 minutes. Invert onto serving plate. Serve warm or at room temperature.

Makes 12 servings

Cranberry Orange Ring

Summer Sausage 'n' Egg Wedges

4 eggs, beaten
⅓ cup milk
¼ cup all-purpose flour
½ teaspoon baking powder
⅛ teaspoon garlic powder
2½ cups (10 ounces) shredded Cheddar or mozzarella cheese, divided
1½ cups diced HILLSHIRE FARM® Summer Sausage
1 cup cream-style cottage cheese with chives

Preheat oven to 375°F.

Combine eggs, milk, flour, baking powder and garlic powder in medium bowl; beat until combined. Stir in 2 cups Cheddar cheese, Summer Sausage and cottage cheese. Pour into greased 9-inch pie plate. Bake, uncovered, 25 to 30 minutes or until golden and knife inserted into center comes out clean. To serve, cut into 6 wedges. Sprinkle wedges with remaining ½ cup Cheddar cheese. *Makes 6 servings*

tip

Cut this egg dish into 8 wedges and serve it on the brunch buffet with assorted muffins, quick breads and fruit juices.

Summer Sausage 'n' Egg Wedge

Cranberry Orange Coffeecake

1½ cups biscuit baking mix
⅓ cup granulated sugar
⅓ cup sour cream
1 egg
1 teaspoon vanilla
2 tablespoons orange juice
1 tablespoon plus 1 teaspoon grated orange peel, divided
1 cup fresh or frozen whole cranberries
½ cup chopped dried fruit (such as apricots, golden raisins and figs)
⅓ cup coarsely chopped walnuts
½ cup brown sugar
2 tablespoons butter, softened
Whipped cream

1. Preheat oven to 350°F. Grease 12-inch tart pan with removable bottom.

2. Stir together baking mix and granulated sugar in large bowl. Beat together sour cream, egg, vanilla, orange juice and 1 tablespoon orange peel in medium bowl. Add sour cream mixture to baking mix and sugar; stir just until moistened. Spread into prepared tart pan.

3. Sprinkle cranberries, dried fruit and walnuts over top of batter. Stir together brown sugar, butter and remaining 1 teaspoon orange peel in small bowl; sprinkle over fruit.

4. Bake 25 to 30 minutes or until lightly browned. Serve warm with whipped cream.

Makes 12 servings

Pumpkin Streusel Coffeecake

Streusel Topping
- ½ **cup all-purpose flour**
- ¼ **cup packed brown sugar**
- 1½ **teaspoons ground cinnamon**
- 3 **tablespoons butter or margarine**
- ½ **cup coarsely chopped nuts**

Coffeecake
- 2 **cups all-purpose flour**
- 2 **teaspoons baking powder**
- 1½ **teaspoons ground cinnamon**
- ½ **teaspoon baking soda**
- ¼ **teaspoon salt**
- 1 **cup (2 sticks) butter or margarine, softened**
- 1 **cup granulated sugar**
- 2 **eggs**
- 1 **cup LIBBY'S® 100% Pure Pumpkin**
- 1 **teaspoon vanilla extract**

PREHEAT oven to 350°F. Grease and flour 9-inch round cake pan.

For Streusel Topping

COMBINE flour, brown sugar and cinnamon in medium bowl. Cut in butter with pastry blender or two knives until mixture is crumbly; stir in nuts.

For Coffeecake

COMBINE flour, baking powder, cinnamon, baking soda and salt in small bowl. Beat butter and granulated sugar in large mixer bowl until creamy. Add eggs, one at a time, beating well after each addition. Beat in pumpkin and vanilla extract. Gradually beat in flour mixture.

SPOON *half* of batter into prepared cake pan. Sprinkle *half* of Streusel Topping over batter. Spoon *remaining* batter evenly over Streusel Topping; sprinkle with *remaining* Streusel Topping.

BAKE for 45 to 50 minutes or until wooden pick inserted into center comes out clean. Cool in pan on wire rack for 10 minutes; remove to wire rack to cool completely.

Makes 10 servings

Green Onion Cream Cheese Breakfast Biscuits

     2 cups all-purpose flour
     1 tablespoon baking powder
     1 tablespoon sugar
     ¾ teaspoon salt
     1 package (3 ounces) cream cheese
     ¼ cup shortening
     ½ cup finely chopped green onions
     ⅔ cup milk

1. Preheat oven to 450°F.

2. Combine flour, baking powder, sugar and salt in medium bowl. Cut in cream cheese and shortening with pastry blender or two knives until mixture resembles coarse crumbs. Stir in green onions.

3. Make well in center of flour mixture. Add milk; stir until mixture forms soft dough that clings together and forms a ball.

4. Turn out dough onto well-floured surface. Knead dough gently 10 to 12 times. Roll or pat dough to ½-inch thickness. Cut dough with floured 3-inch biscuit cutter.

5. Place biscuits 2 inches apart on ungreased large baking sheet. Bake 10 to 12 minutes or until tops and bottoms are golden brown. Serve warm.

Makes 8 biscuits

Serving Suggestion: Serve these savory biscuits at a brunch buffet with a choice of spreads, such as whipped butter, cracked pepper and chive butter, softened butter blended with chopped sun-dried tomatoes packed in oil and drained, or jalapeño jelly.

Green Onion Cream Cheese Breakfast Biscuits

Roasted Red Pepper and Sourdough Brunch Casserole

        3 cups sourdough bread cubes
        1 jar (12 ounces) roasted red pepper strips, drained
        1 cup (4 ounces) shredded reduced-fat sharp Cheddar cheese
        1 cup (4 ounces) shredded reduced-fat Monterey Jack cheese
        1 cup fat-free cottage cheese
    12 ounces cholesterol-free egg substitute
        1 cup fat-free (skim) milk
    ¼ cup chopped fresh cilantro
    ¼ teaspoon black pepper

1. Spray 11×7-inch baking dish with nonstick cooking spray. Place bread cubes in dish. Arrange roasted peppers evenly over bread cubes. Sprinkle Cheddar and Monterey Jack cheeses over peppers.

2. Place cottage cheese in food processor or blender; process until smooth. Add egg substitute; process 10 seconds. Combine cottage cheese mixture and milk in small bowl; pour over ingredients in baking dish. Sprinkle with cilantro and black pepper. Cover; refrigerate 4 to 12 hours.

3. Preheat oven to 375°F. Bake, uncovered, 40 minutes or until hot and bubbly and golden brown on top.   *Makes 8 servings*

Serving Suggestion: Serve with sausage links or Canadian bacon and fresh citrus.

Roasted Red Pepper and Sourdough Brunch Casserole

quick breads & spreads

Cheddar and Apple Muffins

2 cups buttermilk baking mix
½ to 1 teaspoon ground red pepper
½ teaspoon salt
⅔ cup milk
1 egg, lightly beaten
1 medium apple, peeled, cored and grated
1 cup (4 ounces) shredded sharp Cheddar cheese

1. Preheat oven to 375°F. Spray 12 (2½-inch) muffin pan cups with nonstick cooking spray.

2. Combine baking mix, red pepper and salt in large bowl. Add milk and egg; mix until just moistened. *Do not overmix.* Fold in apple and cheese.

3. Spoon batter into prepared muffin cups filling ¾ full. Bake 20 to 25 minutes or until golden brown. Cool 5 minutes in pan. Loosen sides of muffins with knife; remove from pan to wire rack. Serve warm. *Makes 12 muffins*

Chunky Hawaiian Spread

1 package (3 ounces) light cream cheese, softened
½ cup fat free or light sour cream
1 can (8 ounces) DOLE® Crushed Pineapple, well-drained
¼ cup mango chutney*
Low fat crackers

If there are large pieces of fruit in chutney, cut them into small pieces.

• Beat cream cheese, sour cream, crushed pineapple and chutney in bowl until blended. Cover and chill 1 hour or overnight. Serve with crackers. Refrigerate any leftover spread in airtight container for up to one week. *Makes 2½ cups*

Cheddar and Apple Muffins

Mini Pumpkin Cranberry Breads

    3 cups all-purpose flour
    1 tablespoon plus 2 teaspoons pumpkin pie spice
    2 teaspoons baking soda
 1½ teaspoons salt
    3 cups granulated sugar
    1 can (15 ounces) LIBBY'S® 100% Pure Pumpkin
    4 eggs
    1 cup vegetable oil
    ½ cup orange juice or water
    1 cup sweetened dried, fresh or frozen cranberries

PREHEAT oven to 350°F. Grease and flour five or six 5×3-inch mini disposable or meat loaf pans.

COMBINE flour, pumpkin pie spice, baking soda and salt in large bowl. Combine sugar, pumpkin, eggs, vegetable oil and orange juice in large mixer bowl; beat until just blended. Add pumpkin mixture to flour mixture; stir just until moistened. Fold in cranberries. Spoon batter into prepared loaf pans.

BAKE for 50 to 55 minutes or until wooden pick inserted into center comes out clean. Cool in pans on wire racks for 10 minutes; remove to wire racks to cool completely.

Makes 5 or 6 mini loaves

Orange-Cream Spread

    1 package (8 ounces) cream cheese, softened
    3 tablespoons orange marmalade

Beat cream cheese in small bowl on medium speed of electric mixer until smooth. Add marmalade; beat at low speed until blended. Serve with bagels, muffins or quick breads.

Makes about 1 cup

Mini Pumpkin Cranberry Bread

Herb-Cheese Biscuit Loaf

1 ½ cups all-purpose flour
¼ cup grated Parmesan cheese
2 tablespoons yellow cornmeal
2 teaspoons baking powder
½ teaspoon salt
¼ cup butter
2 eggs
½ cup heavy cream
¾ teaspoon dried basil leaves
¾ teaspoon dried oregano leaves
⅛ teaspoon garlic powder
Additional grated Parmesan cheese (optional)

1. Preheat oven to 425°F. Grease large baking sheet; set aside.

2. Combine flour, ¼ cup cheese, cornmeal, baking powder and salt in large bowl. Cut in butter with pastry blender or two knives until mixture resembles coarse crumbs.

3. Beat eggs in medium bowl. Add cream, basil, oregano and garlic powder; beat until well blended. Add cream mixture to flour mixture; stir until mixture forms soft dough that clings together and forms ball.

4. Turn out dough onto well-floured surface. Knead dough gently 10 to 12 times. Place dough on prepared baking sheet. Roll or pat dough into 7-inch round, about 1 inch thick.

5. Starting from center, score top of dough into 8 wedges with tip of sharp knife. (Do not cut completely through dough.) Sprinkle with additional cheese, if desired.

6. Bake 20 to 25 minutes or until toothpick inserted into center comes out clean. Cool on baking sheet on wire rack 10 minutes. Serve warm.   *Makes 8 servings*

Herb-Cheese Biscuit Loaf

Mustard-Pepper Biscuit Ring

2 cups all-purpose flour
1 tablespoon baking powder
1 teaspoon sugar
¾ teaspoon black pepper
½ teaspoon salt
⅛ teaspoon garlic powder
3 tablespoons cold butter or margarine
¾ cup fat-free (skim) milk
2 tablespoons Dijon mustard

1. Preheat oven to 450°F. Lightly spray baking sheet with nonstick cooking spray; set aside.

2. Combine flour, baking powder, sugar, pepper, salt and garlic powder in medium bowl. Cut in butter with pastry blender or two knives until mixture resembles coarse crumbs.

3. Whisk together milk and mustard in small bowl. Add to flour mixture, stirring just until moistened. Drop dough by 14 rounded tablespoonfuls into 9-inch circle on prepared baking sheet, allowing sides of mounds to touch slightly. Bake about 10 minutes or until golden brown. Remove from pan to wire rack.

Makes 14 servings

Prep Time: 10 minutes
Bake Time: 10 minutes

Mustard-Pepper Biscuit Ring

Donna's Heavenly Orange Chip Scones

    4 cups all-purpose flour
    1 cup granulated sugar
    4 teaspoons baking powder
    ½ teaspoon baking soda
    ½ teaspoon salt
    1 cup (6 ounces) NESTLÉ® TOLL HOUSE® Semi-Sweet Chocolate Mini
        Morsels
    1 cup golden raisins
    1 tablespoon grated orange peel
    1 cup (2 sticks) unsalted butter, cut into pieces and softened
    1 cup buttermilk
    3 eggs, *divided*
    1 teaspoon orange extract
    1 tablespoon milk
    Icing (recipe follows)

PREHEAT oven to 350°F. Lightly grease baking sheets.

COMBINE flour, granulated sugar, baking powder, baking soda and salt in large bowl. Add morsels, raisins and orange peel; mix well. Cut in butter with pastry blender or two knives until mixture resembles coarse crumbs. Combine buttermilk, *2 eggs* and orange extract in small bowl. Pour buttermilk mixture into flour mixture; mix just until a sticky dough is formed. Do not overmix. Drop by ¼ cupfuls onto prepared baking sheets. Combine *remaining* egg and milk in small bowl. Brush egg mixture over top of dough.

BAKE for 18 to 22 minutes or until wooden pick inserted into centers comes out clean. For best results, bake one baking sheet at a time. Cool on wire racks for 10 minutes. Drizzle scones with icing. Serve warm.   *Makes 2 dozen scones*

Icing: COMBINE 2 cups powdered sugar, ¼ cup orange juice, 1 tablespoon grated orange peel and 1 teaspoon orange extract in medium bowl. Mix until smooth.

Donna's Heavenly Orange Chip Scones

Cherry Zucchini Bread

2 eggs
¾ cup sugar
⅓ cup vegetable oil
⅓ cup lemon juice
¼ cup water
2 cups all-purpose flour
2 teaspoons baking powder
1 teaspoon ground cinnamon
½ teaspoon baking soda
¼ teaspoon salt
⅔ cup shredded unpeeled zucchini
⅔ cup dried tart cherries
1 tablespoon grated lemon peel

Put eggs in large mixing bowl. Beat with an electric mixer on medium speed 3 to 4 minutes or until eggs are thick and lemon colored. Add sugar, oil, lemon juice and water; mix well. Combine flour, baking powder, cinnamon, baking soda and salt. Add flour mixture to egg mixture; mix well. Stir in zucchini, cherries and lemon peel.

Grease and flour bottom of 8½×4½-inch loaf pan. Pour batter into prepared pan. Bake in preheated 350°F oven 55 to 65 minutes or until wooden toothpick inserted into center comes out clean. Let cool in pan on wire rack 10 minutes. Loosen edges with a metal spatula. Remove from pan. Let cool completely. Wrap tightly in plastic wrap and store in refrigerator. *Makes 1 loaf, about 16 servings*

Favorite recipe from **Cherry Marketing Institute**

Focaccia with Dried Tomatoes and Fontina

1 tablespoon olive oil
1 loaf (1 pound) frozen bread dough, thawed according to package directions
1 jar (8 ounces) SONOMA® Marinated Dried Tomatoes, drained and 2 tablespoons oil reserved
4 cloves garlic, minced
⅔ cup sliced black olives
1 tablespoon dried basil
1 teaspoon dried oregano
1 teaspoon dried rosemary
2 cups shredded fontina cheese

Preheat oven to 425°F. Oil 13×9×2-inch baking pan. Roll and stretch dough on lightly floured surface; fit dough into pan.

Combine reserved tomato oil with garlic; brush over dough. Sprinkle olives, basil, oregano and rosemary evenly over dough. Arrange tomatoes on top; cover with cheese.

Bake for 35 to 40 minutes until bread is springy to the touch and golden brown around edges. (Cover loosely with foil during last 10 minutes if becoming too brown.) Cut into squares while still warm.   *Makes 16 squares*

English-Style Scones

3 eggs
½ cup heavy cream
1½ teaspoons vanilla
2 cups all-purpose flour
2 teaspoons baking powder
¼ teaspoon salt
¼ cup cold butter
¼ cup finely chopped pitted dates
¼ cup golden raisins or currants
1 teaspoon water
6 tablespoons no-sugar-added orange marmalade fruit spread
6 tablespoons softly whipped cream or crème fraîche

1. Preheat oven to 375°F. Beat 2 eggs with cream and vanilla; set aside.

2. Combine flour, baking powder and salt in medium bowl. Cut in butter with pastry blender or two knives until mixture resembles coarse crumbs. Stir in dates and raisins. Add cream mixture; mix just until dry ingredients are moistened.

3. With floured hands, knead dough four times on lightly floured surface. Place dough on greased cookie sheet; pat into 8-inch circle. With sharp wet knife, gently score dough into six wedges, cutting ¾ of the way into dough. Beat remaining egg with water; brush lightly over dough.

4. Bake 18 to 20 minutes or until golden brown. Cool 5 minutes on wire rack. Cut into wedges. Serve warm with marmalade and whipped cream.   *Makes 6 scones*

English-Style Scone

Lemon Poppy Seed Muffins

3 cups all-purpose flour
1 cup sugar
3 tablespoons poppy seeds
1 tablespoon grated lemon peel
2 teaspoons baking powder
1 teaspoon baking soda
½ teaspoon salt
1 container (16 ounces) plain low-fat yogurt
½ cup fresh lemon juice
2 eggs, beaten
¼ cup vegetable oil
1½ teaspoons vanilla

1. Preheat oven to 400°F. Lightly grease 12 large (3½-inch) muffin cups or line with paper baking cups.

2. Combine flour, sugar, poppy seeds, lemon peel, baking powder, baking soda and salt in large bowl; stir until blended. Combine yogurt, lemon juice, eggs, oil and vanilla in small bowl; stir until well blended. Stir yogurt mixture into flour mixture just until moistened. Spoon batter into prepared muffin cups, filling ⅔ full.

3. Bake 25 to 30 minutes or until toothpicks inserted into centers come out clean. Cool in pans on wire racks 5 minutes. Remove from pans. Cool on wire racks 10 minutes. Serve warm or cool completely.

Makes 12 large muffins

Lemon Poppy Seed Muffins

Greek Spinach-Cheese Rolls

1 loaf (1 pound) frozen bread dough
1 package (10 ounces) frozen chopped spinach, thawed and
squeezed dry
¾ cup (3 ounces) crumbled feta cheese
½ cup (2 ounces) shredded reduced-fat Monterey Jack cheese
4 green onions, thinly sliced
1 teaspoon dried dill weed
½ teaspoon garlic powder
½ teaspoon black pepper

1. Thaw bread dough according to package directions. Spray 15 muffin cups with nonstick cooking spray; set aside. Roll out dough on lightly floured surface to 15×9-inch rectangle. (If dough is springy and difficult to roll, cover with plastic wrap and let rest 5 minutes to relax.) Position dough so long edge runs parallel to edge of work surface.

2. Combine spinach, cheeses, green onions, dill weed, garlic powder and pepper in large bowl; mix well.

3. Sprinkle spinach mixture evenly over dough to within 1 inch of long edges. Starting at long edge, roll up snugly, pinching seam closed. Place seam side down; cut roll with serrated knife into 1-inch-wide slices. Place slices, cut sides up, in prepared muffin cups. Cover with plastic wrap; let stand 30 minutes in warm place until rolls are slightly puffy.

4. Preheat oven to 375°F. Bake 20 to 25 minutes or until golden. Serve warm or at room temperature. Rolls can be stored in refrigerator in airtight container up to 2 days. Garnish, if desired. *Makes 15 rolls*

Greek Spinach-Cheese Rolls

Zucchini-Orange Bread

1 package (about 17 ounces) cranberry-orange muffin mix
1½ cups shredded zucchini (about 6 ounces)
1 cup water
1 teaspoon ground cinnamon
1 teaspoon grated orange peel (optional)
Cream cheese (optional)

1. Preheat oven 350°F. Grease 8×4×3-inch loaf pan; set aside.

2. Combine muffin mix, zucchini, water, cinnamon and orange peel, if desired, in medium bowl; stir until just moistened. Spoon batter into prepared loaf pan; bake 40 minutes or until toothpick inserted into center comes out almost clean.

3. Cool in pan on wire rack 5 minutes. Remove bread from pan to wire rack; cool completely. Serve plain or with cream cheese, if desired.   *Makes about 16 slices*

Cherry Orange Poppy Seed Muffins

2 cups all-purpose flour
¾ cup granulated sugar
1 tablespoon baking powder
1 tablespoon poppy seeds
¼ teaspoon salt
1 cup milk
¼ cup (½ stick) butter, melted
1 egg, lightly beaten
½ cup dried tart cherries
3 tablespoons grated orange peel

Combine flour, sugar, baking powder, poppy seeds and salt in large mixing bowl. Add milk, melted butter and egg, stirring just until dry ingredients are moistened. Gently stir in cherries and orange peel. Fill paper-lined muffin cups three-fourths full.

Bake in preheated 400°F oven 18 to 22 minutes or until wooden pick inserted into center comes out clean. Let cool in pan 5 minutes. Remove from pan and serve warm or let cool completely.   *Makes 12 muffins*

Favorite recipe from **Cherry Marketing Institute**

Zucchini-Orange Bread

Blueberry Oats Muffins

⅓ cup sugar
¼ cup margarine or butter, softened
1 egg
1 cup all-purpose flour
¾ cup whole wheat flour
¾ cup uncooked oats (quick-cooking or old-fashioned)
4 teaspoons baking powder
½ teaspoon baking soda
½ teaspoon salt
1 cup buttermilk
1 teaspoon vanilla extract
1½ cups fresh or frozen blueberries, thawed and well drained
Topping (recipe follows)

Cream sugar and margarine until light and fluffy; add egg and beat until smooth. Mix flours, oats, baking powder, soda and salt together; add alternately with buttermilk, stirring well after each addition. Add vanilla extract and fold in blueberries. Spoon batter into greased muffin cups, dividing batter to make 12 large or 18 medium muffins. Sprinkle topping on top of muffin batter. Bake at 375°F for 25 to 30 minutes.

Makes 12 large or 18 medium muffins

Topping

¼ cup all-purpose flour
¼ cup sugar
2 tablespoons melted margarine
½ teaspoon ground cinnamon

Mix ingredients together until crumbly.

*Favorite recipe from **North Dakota Wheat Commission***

Lemon Bread

1 ¼ **cups sugar, divided**
⅓ **cup margarine**
2 **teaspoons grated lemon peel**
2 **eggs**
1 ½ **cups all-purpose flour**
1 **teaspoon baking powder**
¼ **teaspoon salt**
½ **cup milk**
2 **to 3 tablespoons lemon juice**

Cream ¾ cup sugar, margarine and lemon peel. Add eggs; beat well. Sift together flour, baking powder and salt. Mix flour mixture into batter alternately with milk, beginning and ending with flour mixture.

Pour into 8×4-inch loaf pan coated with nonstick cooking spray. Bake at 325°F for 50 to 60 minutes. Mix lemon juice and remaining ½ cup sugar thoroughly. Pour over bread while still hot. Let set in pan 5 to 10 minutes. Remove from pan and cool on cooling rack.   *Makes 1 loaf (18 slices)*

Favorite recipe from **North Dakota Wheat Commission**

sweet endings

Chocolate Lava Cakes

6 tablespoons I CAN'T BELIEVE IT'S NOT BUTTER!® Spread
3 squares (1 ounce each) bittersweet or semi-sweet chocolate,
   cut into pieces
½ cup granulated sugar
6 tablespoons all-purpose flour
   Pinch salt
2 eggs
2 egg yolks
¼ teaspoon vanilla extract
   Confectioners' sugar

Line bottom of four (4-ounce) ramekins* or custard cups with waxed paper, then grease; set aside.

In medium microwave-safe bowl, microwave I Can't Believe It's Not Butter!® Spread and chocolate at HIGH (Full Power) 45 seconds or until chocolate is melted; stir until smooth. With wire whisk, beat in granulated sugar, flour and salt until blended. Beat in eggs, egg yolks and vanilla. Evenly spoon into prepared ramekins. Refrigerate 1 hour or until ready to bake.

Preheat oven to 425°F. Arrange ramekins on baking sheet. Bake 13 minutes or until edges are firm but centers are still slightly soft. *Do not overbake.* On wire rack, cool 5 minutes. To serve, carefully run sharp knife around cake edges. Unmold onto serving plates, then remove waxed paper. Sprinkle with confectioners' sugar and serve immediately.   *Makes 4 servings*

*To bake in 12-cup muffin pan, line bottoms of 8 muffin cups with waxed paper, then grease. Evenly spoon in batter. Refrigerate as above. Bake at 425°F for 9 minutes or until edges are firm but centers are still slightly soft. Do not overbake. On wire rack, cool 5 minutes. To serve, carefully run sharp knife around cake edges and gently lift out of pan. (Do not turn pan upside-down to unmold.) Arrange cakes, bottom sides up, on serving plates, 2 cakes per serving. Remove waxed paper and sprinkle as above.

Chocolate Lava Cake

Summertime Fruit Medley

2 large ripe peaches, peeled and sliced
2 large ripe nectarines, sliced
1 large ripe mango, peeled and cut into 1-inch chunks
1 cup blueberries
2 cups orange juice
¼ cup amaretto *or* ½ teaspoon almond extract
2 tablespoons sugar

1. Combine peaches, nectarines, mango and blueberries in large bowl.

2. Whisk orange juice, amaretto and sugar in small bowl until sugar is dissolved. Pour over fruit mixture; toss. Marinate 1 hour at room temperature, gently stirring occasionally. Garnish with fresh mint, if desired.   *Makes 8 servings*

Sautéed Mangoes & Peaches with Peanut Brittle Topping

2 tablespoons butter
2 large ripe peaches, cut into wedges
1 medium ripe mango, peeled and sliced
1 tablespoon brown sugar
4 scoops vanilla ice cream
½ cup peanut brittle, crushed

1. Melt butter over medium-high heat in large nonstick skillet Add peach and mango slices; sprinkle with brown sugar. Cook and stir gently 3 to 4 minutes or until heated through and fruits begin to soften.

2. Divide fruits equally among 4 individual dessert bowls. Top each with 1 scoop ice cream and peanut brittle.   *Makes 4 servings*

Tip: Purchased mango slices in light syrup packed in jars can be substituted for fresh mango slices. Look for them in refrigerated area of the supermarket produce section. Drain them well before using.

Prep and Cook Time: 17 minutes

Summertime Fruit Medley

Thumbprints

1 package (20 ounces) refrigerated sugar or chocolate cookie dough
All-purpose flour (optional)
¾ cup plus 1 tablespoon fruit preserves, any flavor

1. Grease cookie sheets. Remove dough from wrapper according to package directions. Sprinkle with flour to minimize sticking, if necessary.

2. Cut dough into 26 (1-inch) slices; shape into balls, sprinkling with additional flour, if necessary. Place balls 2 inches apart on prepared cookie sheets. Press deep indentation in center of each ball with thumb. Freeze dough 20 minutes.

3. Preheat oven to 350°F. Bake cookies 12 to 13 minutes or until edges are light golden brown (cookies will have started to puff up and lose their shape). Quickly press down indentation using tip of teaspoon.

4. Return to oven 2 to 3 minutes or until cookies are golden brown and set. Cool cookies completely on cookie sheets. Fill each indentation with about 1½ teaspoons preserves. *Makes 26 cookies*

Tip: These cookies are just as delicious filled with peanut butter or melted semisweet chocolate chips.

Spicy Lemon Crescents

1 cup (2 sticks) butter or margarine, softened
1½ cups powdered sugar, divided
½ teaspoon lemon extract
½ teaspoon grated lemon peel
2 cups cake flour
½ cup finely chopped almonds, walnuts or pecans
1 teaspoon ground cinnamon
½ teaspoon ground cardamom
½ teaspoon ground nutmeg
1¾ cups "M&M's"® Chocolate Mini Baking Bits

Preheat oven to 375°F. Lightly grease cookie sheets; set aside. In large bowl cream butter and ½ cup sugar; add lemon extract and peel, beating until well blended. In medium bowl combine flour, nuts, cinnamon, cardamom and nutmeg; add to creamed mixture, beating until well blended. Stir in "M&M's"® Chocolate Mini Baking Bits. Using 1 tablespoon of dough at a time, form into crescent shapes; place about 2 inches apart onto prepared cookie sheets. Bake 12 to 14 minutes or until edges are golden. Cool 2 minutes on cookie sheets. Gently roll warm crescents in remaining 1 cup sugar. Cool completely on wire racks. Store in tightly covered container.

Makes about 2 dozen cookies

Gingerbread People

½ cup butter, softened
½ cup packed brown sugar
⅓ cup molasses
⅓ cup water
1 egg
4 cups all-purpose flour
2 teaspoons baking soda
1 teaspoon ground ginger
½ teaspoon ground allspice
½ teaspoon ground cinnamon
½ teaspoon ground cloves
White or colored frostings

Beat butter and brown sugar in large bowl with electric mixer at medium speed until creamy. Add molasses, water and egg; beat until blended. Stir in flour, baking soda, ginger, allspice, cinnamon and cloves until well blended. Cover; refrigerate about 2 hours or until firm.

Preheat oven to 350°F. Grease cookie sheets. Roll out dough to ⅛-inch thickness on lightly floured surface with lightly floured rolling pin. Cut with cookie cutter. Place 2 inches apart on prepared cookie sheets.

Bake 12 to 15 minutes or until firm to the touch. Cool 1 minute on cookie sheets. Remove to wire racks; cool completely. Decorate with frostings. Store in airtight containers.

Makes about 4½ dozen cookies

Berry-Berry Brownie Torte

½ cup all-purpose flour
¼ teaspoon baking soda
¼ teaspoon salt
1 cup HERSHEY'S Raspberry Chips or HERSHEY'S Semi-Sweet
    Chocolate Chips
½ cup (1 stick) butter or margarine
1¼ cups sugar, divided
2 eggs
1 teaspoon vanilla extract
⅓ cup HERSHEY'S Dutch Processed Cocoa
½ cup whipping cream
¾ cup fresh blackberries, rinsed and patted dry
¾ cup fresh raspberries, rinsed and patted dry

1. Heat oven to 350°F. Line 9-inch round baking pan with wax paper, then grease. Stir together flour, baking soda and salt. Stir in raspberry chips.

2. Melt butter in medium saucepan over low heat. Remove from heat. Stir in 1 cup sugar, eggs and vanilla. Add cocoa, blending well. Stir in flour mixture. Spread mixture in prepared pan.

3. Bake 20 to 25 minutes or until wooden pick inserted into center comes out slightly sticky. Cool in pan on wire rack 15 minutes. Invert onto wire rack; remove wax paper. Turn right side up; cool completely.

4. Beat whipping cream and remaining ¼ cup sugar until sugar is dissolved and stiff peaks form. Spread over top of brownie. Top with berries. Refrigerate until serving time.
Makes 8 to 10 servings

Berry-Berry Brownie Torte

Apple-Walnut Glazed Spice Baby Cakes

   1 package (about 18 ounces) spice cake mix
1⅓ cups plus 3 tablespoons water, divided
   3 eggs
   ⅓ cup vegetable oil
   ½ teaspoon vanilla butter and nut flavoring*
   ¾ cup chopped walnuts
   12 ounces Granny Smith apples, peeled and cut into ½-inch cubes
   ¼ teaspoon ground cinnamon
   1 jar (12 ounces) caramel ice cream topping

*Vanilla butter and nut flavoring is available in the baking section of most large supermarkets. Vanilla may be substituted.

1. Preheat oven to 350°F. Lightly grease and flour 12 (1-cup) mini bundt pans.

2. Beat cake mix, 1⅓ cups water, eggs, oil and flavoring in large bowl 30 seconds on low speed of electric mixer. Beat 2 minutes at medium speed.

3. Spoon batter evenly into prepared pans. Bake 25 minutes or until toothpick inserted near centers of cakes comes out almost clean. Cool in pans on wire rack 15 minutes. Carefully invert cakes from pans to wire rack; cool completely.

4. Meanwhile, place 12-inch skillet over medium high heat until hot. Add walnuts; cook 3 minutes or until walnuts are lightly browned, stirring frequently. Remove nuts to small bowl. In same skillet, combine apples, remaining 3 tablespoons water and cinnamon; cook and stir over medium-high heat 3 minutes or until apples are crisp-tender. Remove from heat; stir in walnuts and caramel topping. Spoon glaze over each cake.   *Makes 12 cakes*

Apple-Walnut Glazed Spice Baby Cakes

Pumpkin Pecan Rum Cake

¾ cup chopped pecans
3 cups all-purpose flour
2 tablespoons pumpkin pie spice
2 teaspoons baking soda
1 teaspoon salt
1 cup (2 sticks) butter or margarine, softened
1 cup packed brown sugar
1 cup granulated sugar
4 eggs
1 can (15 ounces) LIBBY'S® 100% Pure Pumpkin
1 teaspoon vanilla extract
    Rum Butter Glaze (recipe follows)

PREHEAT oven to 325°F. Grease 12-cup Bundt pan. Sprinkle nuts over bottom.

COMBINE flour, pumpkin pie spice, baking soda and salt in medium bowl. Beat butter, brown sugar and granulated sugar in large mixer bowl until light and fluffy. Add eggs; beat well. Add pumpkin and vanilla extract; beat well. Add flour mixture to pumpkin mixture, ⅓ at a time, mixing well after each addition. Spoon batter into prepared pan.

BAKE for 60 to 70 minutes or until wooden pick comes out clean. Cool 10 minutes. Make holes in cake with long pick; pour *half* of glaze over cake. Let stand 5 minutes and invert onto plate. Make holes in top of cake; pour *remaining* glaze over cake. Cool. Garnish as desired.   *Makes 24 servings*

Rum Butter Glaze: MELT ¼ cup butter or margarine in small saucepan; stir in ½ cup granulated sugar and 2 tablespoons water. Bring to a boil. Remove from heat; stir in 2 to 3 tablespoons dark rum or 1 teaspoon rum extract.

Pumpkin Pecan Rum Cake

Stars and Stripes Cupcakes

42 cupcakes, any flavor
2 containers (16 ounces each) vanilla frosting
Fresh blueberries, washed and dried
Fresh strawberries, washed, dried, stemmed and halved

1. Frost cupcakes with vanilla frosting.

2. Decorate 9 cupcakes with blueberries, leaving space between the blueberries. Decorate remaining cupcakes with strawberry halves, placing each strawberry half at edge of cupcake as shown in photo.

3. Arrange cupcakes on a rectangular tray or on table to form flag: Place blueberry-topped cupcakes in the upper left part of the tray and the strawberry-topped cupcakes in rows to resemble red and white stripes of the flag. *Makes 42 servings*

Easy Chocolate Cheese Pie

2 bars (1 ounce each) HERSHEY'S Unsweetened Baking Chocolate, broken into pieces
¼ cup (½ stick) butter or margarine, softened
¾ cup sugar
1 package (3 ounces) cream cheese, softened
1 teaspoon milk
2 cups frozen whipped topping, thawed
1 packaged crumb crust (6 ounces)
Additional whipped topping (optional)

1. Place chocolate in small microwave-safe bowl. Microwave at HIGH (100%) 1 to 1½ minutes or until chocolate is melted and smooth when stirred.

2. Beat butter, sugar, cream cheese and milk in medium bowl until well blended and smooth; fold in melted chocolate.

3. Fold in 2 cups whipped topping; spoon into crust. Cover; refrigerate until firm, about 3 hours. Garnish with additional whipped topping, if desired.
Makes 6 to 8 servings

Stars and Stripes Cupcakes

Premier White Lemony Cheesecake

Crust
>   6 tablespoons butter or margarine, softened
>   ¼ cup granulated sugar
>   1 ¼ cups all-purpose flour
>   1 egg yolk
>   ⅛ teaspoon salt

Filling
>   6 bars (*two* 6-ounce boxes) NESTLÉ® TOLL HOUSE® Premier White
>   Baking Bars, broken into pieces or 2 cups (12-ounce package)
>   NESTLÉ® TOLL HOUSE® Premier White Morsels
>   ½ cup heavy whipping cream
>   2 packages (8 ounces *each*) cream cheese, softened
>   1 tablespoon lemon juice
>   2 teaspoons grated lemon peel
>   ¼ teaspoon salt
>   3 egg whites
>   1 egg

PREHEAT oven to 350°F. Lightly grease 9-inch springform pan.

For Crust

BEAT butter and sugar in small mixer bowl until creamy. Beat in flour, egg yolk and salt. Press mixture onto bottom and 1 inch up side of prepared pan.

BAKE for 14 to 16 minutes or until crust is set.

For Filling

MICROWAVE baking bars and whipping cream in medium, uncovered, microwave-safe bowl on MEDIUM-HIGH (70%) power for 1 minute. STIR. Morsels may retain some of their original shape. If necessary, microwave at additional 10- to 15-second intervals, stirring just until morsels are melted.

BEAT cream cheese, lemon juice, lemon peel and salt in large mixer bowl until smooth. Gradually beat in melted baking bars. Beat in egg whites and egg. Pour into crust.

BAKE for 35 to 40 minutes or until edge is lightly browned. Run knife around edge of cheesecake. Cool completely in pan on wire rack. Refrigerate for several hours or overnight. Remove side of springform pan. Garnish as desired.

Makes 12 to 16 servings

Premier White Lemony Cheesecake

Chunky Caramel Nut Brownies

4 squares (1 ounce each) unsweetened chocolate
¾ cup (1½ sticks) butter
2 cups sugar
4 eggs
1 cup all-purpose flour
1 package (14 ounces) caramels
¼ cup heavy cream
2 cups pecan halves or coarsely chopped pecans, divided
1 package (12 ounces) chocolate chunks or chips

1. Preheat oven to 350°F. Grease 13×9-inch baking pan; set aside.

2. Place chocolate and butter in large microwavable bowl. Microwave at HIGH 1½ to 2 minutes or until chocolate is melted and mixture is smooth when stirred. Stir in sugar until well blended. Beat in eggs, 1 at a time. Stir in flour until well blended. Spread half of batter in prepared pan. Bake 20 minutes.

3. Meanwhile, combine caramels and cream in medium microwavable bowl. Microwave at HIGH 1½ to 2 minutes or until caramels begin to melt; stir until mixture is smooth. Stir in 1 cup pecan halves.

4. Spread caramel mixture over partially baked brownie. Sprinkle with half of chocolate chunks. Pour remaining brownie batter over top; sprinkle with remaining 1 cup pecan halves and chocolate chunks. Bake 25 to 30 minutes or until set. Cool in pan on wire rack.

Makes 2 dozen brownies

Chunky Caramel Nut Brownies

Sweet Showers

1 cup unsalted butter, softened
½ cup sugar
1 teaspoon lemon extract
1 teaspoon orange extract
½ teaspoon vanilla
2½ cups all-purpose flour
⅛ teaspoon salt
Assorted icings, colored sprinkles, sugars and decors

1. Beat butter, sugar, lemon extract, orange extract and vanilla in large bowl at medium speed of electric mixer until creamy. Stir in flour and salt until well blended. (Dough will be crumbly.) Knead dough into smooth ball.

2. Preheat oven to 350°F. Lightly grease cookie sheets. Roll out dough, small portion at a time, to ¼-inch thickness on floured surface with lightly floured rolling pin. Cut out dough with 3-inch umbrella-shaped cookie cutter. Transfer to prepared cookie sheets.

3. Bake 12 to 14 minutes or until edges are lightly browned. Let cookies stand on cookie sheets 1 to 2 minutes; transfer to wire racks to cool completely. Decorate cookies with pink and blue icings and sprinkles for baby shower, or colors to match wedding for bridal shower. Let stand until icing is set.   *Makes 2 dozen cookies*

tip

These delightful cookies will win raves at baby or bridal showers. Look for the fancy sprinkles at large supermarkets, specialty food shops or craft stores.

Tempting Chocolate Mousse

1 envelope unflavored gelatin
2½ cups nonfat milk
¼ cup HERSHEY'S Cocoa or HERSHEY'S Dutch Processed Cocoa
1 tablespoon cornstarch
1 egg yolk
1 teaspoon vanilla extract
Granulated sugar substitute to equal 8 teaspoons sugar
1 cup prepared sucrose-free whipped topping*

Prepare 1 envelope (1 ounce) sucrose-free dry whipped topping mix with ½ cup very cold water according to package directions. (This makes about 2 cups topping; use 1 cup topping for mousse. Reserve remainder for garnish, if desired.)

1. Sprinkle gelatin over milk in medium saucepan; let stand 5 minutes to soften. Stir in cocoa, cornstarch and egg yolk; cook over medium heat, stirring constantly with whisk, until mixture comes to a boil. Reduce heat to low; cook, stirring constantly, until mixture thickens slightly, about 1 minute.

2. Remove from heat; cool to lukewarm. Stir in vanilla and sugar substitute. Pour mixture into medium bowl. Refrigerate, stirring occasionally, until thickened, about 45 minutes.

3. Fold 1 cup prepared whipped topping into chocolate mixture. Spoon into 6 individual dessert dishes. Cover; refrigerate until firm. Garnish with remaining whipped topping, if desired.   *Makes 6 servings*

Tempting Chocolate Mousse

Reese's® Peanut Butter and Milk Chocolate Chip Blondies

1½ cups packed light brown sugar
1 cup (2 sticks) butter or margarine, melted
½ cup sugar
2 eggs
2 teaspoons vanilla extract
2 cups all-purpose flour
1 teaspoon salt
1¾ cups (11-ounce package) REESE'S® Peanut Butter and Milk
  Chocolate Chips, divided
¼ teaspoon shortening (do not use butter, margarine, spread or oil)

1. Heat oven to 350°F. Grease 15½×10½×1-inch jelly-roll pan.

2. Stir together brown sugar, butter and granulated sugar in large bowl; beat in eggs and vanilla. Add flour and salt, beating just until blended. Stir in 1½ cups chips; spread batter in prepared pan.

3. Bake 25 to 30 minutes or until wooden pick inserted in center comes out clean and surface is lightly browned. Cool completely; cut into bars.

4. Place remaining ¼ cup chips and shortening in small microwave-safe bowl. Microwave at HIGH (100%) 30 seconds; stir. If necessary, microwave at HIGH an additional 15 seconds at a time, stirring after each heating, until chips are melted and mixture is smooth when stirred. Drizzle over bars.   *Makes about 6 dozen bars*

Reese's® Peanut Butter and Milk Chocolate Chip Blondies

Holiday Cheese Tarts

1 (8-ounce) package cream cheese, softened
1 (14-ounce) can EAGLE BRAND® Sweetened Condensed Milk
    (NOT evaporated milk)
⅓ cup lemon juice from concentrate
1 teaspoon vanilla extract
2 (4-ounce) packages single-serve graham cracker crumb pie crusts
    Assorted fruit (strawberries, blueberries, bananas, raspberries,
        orange segments, cherries, kiwi fruit, grapes, pineapple, etc.)
¼ cup apple jelly, melted (optional)

1. In medium mixing bowl, beat cream cheese until fluffy. Gradually beat in EAGLE BRAND® until smooth. Stir in lemon juice and vanilla.

2. Spoon into crusts. Chill 2 hours or until set. Just before serving, top with fruit; brush with jelly, if desired. Refrigerate leftovers.   *Makes 12 tarts*

Prep Time: 10 minutes
Chill Time: 2 hours

tip

These tarts are a colorful addition to a buffet. They can be made a day ahead, covered and chilled overnight. Decorate them with beautiful looking fruit a few hours before serving them.

Moons and Stars

1 cup butter, softened
1 cup sugar
1 egg
2 teaspoons lemon peel
½ teaspoon almond extract
3 cups all-purpose flour
½ cup ground almonds
  Assorted colored decorating icings, hard candies and colored sprinkles

1. Preheat oven to 350°F. Grease cookie sheets.

2. Beat butter, sugar, egg, lemon peel and almond extract in large bowl at medium speed of electric mixer until light and fluffy.

3. Combine flour and almonds in medium bowl. Add flour mixture to butter mixture; stir just until combined.

4. Roll dough on lightly floured surface to ⅛- to ¼-inch thickness. Cut out cookies using moon and star cookie cutters. Place cookies 2 inches apart on prepared cookie sheets.

5. Bake 7 to 9 minutes or until set but not browned. Cool on cookie sheets 2 minutes. Remove to wire racks; cool completely.

6. Decorate cookies with icings, candies and sprinkles as desired.

Makes about 4 dozen cookies

Triple Chocolate Cake

1½ cups sugar
¾ cup butter, softened
1 egg
1 teaspoon vanilla
2 cups all-purpose flour
⅔ cup unsweetened cocoa powder
2 teaspoons baking soda
¼ teaspoon salt
1 cup buttermilk
¾ cup sour cream
    Chocolate Ganache Filling (recipe follows)
    Easy Chocolate Frosting (recipe follows)

1. Preheat oven to 350°F. Grease and flour two 9-inch round cake pans. Beat sugar and butter at medium speed of electric mixer until light and fluffy. Beat in egg and vanilla until blended. Combine flour, cocoa, baking soda and salt in medium bowl. Add flour mixture to butter mixture alternately with buttermilk and sour cream, beginning and ending with flour mixture. Beat well after each addition. Divide batter evenly between prepared pans.

2. Bake 30 to 35 minutes or until wooden toothpick inserted into centers comes out clean. Cool in pans 10 minutes. Remove from pans to wire racks; cool completely. Cut each cake layer in half horizontally.

3. Meanwhile, prepare Chocolate Ganache Filling and Easy Chocolate Frosting. Place one cake layer on serving plate. Spread with ⅓ of filling. Repeat layers two more times. Top with remaining cake layer. Spread frosting over top and side of cake. Garnish as desired.   *Makes 1 (9-inch) layer cake*

Chocolate Ganache Filling: Bring ¾ cup heavy cream, 1 tablespoon butter and 1 tablespoon granulated sugar to a boil; stir until sugar is dissolved. Place 1½ cups semisweet chocolate chips in medium bowl; pour cream mixture over chocolate and let stand 5 minutes. Stir until smooth; let stand 15 minutes or until filling reaches desired consistency. (Filling will thicken as it cools.) Makes about 1½ cups.

Easy Chocolate Frosting: Beat ½ cup (1 stick) softened butter in large bowl with electric mixer at medium speed until creamy. Add 4 cups powdered sugar and ¾ cup cocoa alternately with ½ cup milk; beat until smooth. Stir in 1½ teaspoons vanilla. Makes about 3 cups.

Triple Chocolate Cake

Bananas Foster

6 tablespoons I CAN'T BELIEVE IT'S NOT BUTTER!® Spread
3 tablespoons firmly packed brown sugar
4 medium ripe bananas, sliced diagonally
2 tablespoons dark rum or brandy (optional)
   Vanilla ice cream

In 12-inch skillet, bring I Can't Believe It's Not Butter!® Spread, brown sugar and bananas to a boil. Cook 2 minutes, stirring gently. Carefully add rum to center of pan and cook 15 seconds. Serve hot banana mixture over scoops of ice cream and top, if desired, with sweetened whipped cream. *Makes 4 servings*

Note: Recipe can be halved.

Prep Time: 5 minutes
Cook Time: 5 minutes

Easy Mocha Brownies

2 tablespoons instant espresso powder
2 tablespoons hot water
1 cup (2 sticks) butter
¾ cup packed brown sugar
⅔ cup granulated sugar
3 eggs, lightly beaten
1 cup all-purpose flour
⅔ cup unsweetened cocoa powder
½ teaspoon salt
½ teaspoon baking powder

1. Preheat oven to 350°F. Grease 13×9-inch baking pan; set aside. Dissolve espresso powder in water; cool.

2. Melt butter in saucepan over low heat; cool slightly. Beat in sugars, eggs and espresso liquid. Stir in combined flour, cocoa, salt and baking powder until blended.

3. Spread batter into prepared pan. Bake 30 to 32 minutes or until toothpick inserted into center comes out clean. Cool completely on wire rack. Sprinkle with sifted powdered sugar, if desired. *Makes 24 brownies*

Bananas Foster

Wedding Bells

1 cup unsalted butter, softened
¾ cup sugar
2 eggs
2½ cups all-purpose flour
1 teaspoon baking powder
¼ teaspoon salt
¼ teaspoon ground cinnamon
Assorted icings, colored sprinkles, sugars and decors
Thin ribbon

1. Beat butter and sugar in large bowl at medium speed of electric mixer until creamy. Add eggs; beat until fluffy. Stir in flour, baking powder, salt and cinnamon until well blended. Form dough into ball; wrap in plastic wrap and flatten. Refrigerate about 2 hours or until firm.

2. Preheat oven to 350°F. Lightly grease cookie sheets. Roll out dough, small portion at a time, to ¼-inch thickness on floured surface with lightly floured rolling pin. (Keep remaining dough wrapped in refrigerator.) Cut out dough with 2½-inch bell-shaped cookie cutter. Transfer to prepared cookie sheets. Make small hole in top of each bell with tip of drinking straw.

3. Bake 10 to 12 minutes or until edges are lightly browned. Let cookies stand on cookie sheets 1 minute; transfer to wire racks to cool completely. Decorate cookies with icings, sprinkles, sugars and decors to match wedding colors. Tie 2 bells together with ribbon.   *Makes 3 dozen cookies*

tip

These cookies make eye-catching party favors for a bridal shower or anniversary party.

Wedding Bells

Acknowledgments

The publisher would like to thank the companies and organizations listed below for the use of their recipes and photographs in this publication.

Bays English Muffin Corporation

Alouette® Cheese, Chavrie® Cheese, Saladena®

BelGioioso® Cheese, Inc.

Cherry Marketing Institute

Clamato® is a registered trademark of Mott's, LLP

Delmarva Poultry Industry, Inc.

Dole Food Company, Inc.

Eagle Brand® Sweetened Condensed Milk

Florida Department of Agriculture and Consumer Services, Bureau of Seafood and Aquaculture

The Golden Grain Company®

Hebrew National®

Hershey Foods Corporation

The Hidden Valley® Food Products Company

Hillshire Farm®

Hormel Foods, Carapelli USA, LLC and Melting Pot Foods Inc.

Hormel Foods, LLC

Jennie-O Turkey Store®

The Kingsford® Products Co.

Lawry's® Foods

© Mars, Incorporated 2005

MASTERFOODS USA

McIlhenny Company (TABASCO® brand Pepper Sauce)

National Honey Board

Nestlé USA

Norseland, Inc. Lucini Italia Co.

North Dakota Wheat Commission

Perdue Farms Incorporated

Reckitt Benckiser Inc.

Riviana Foods Inc.

Sargento® Foods Inc.

Sonoma® Dried Tomatoes

Reprinted with permission of Sunkist Growers, Inc.

Unilever Foods North America

US Highbush Blueberry Council

Index

METRIC CONVERSION CHART

VOLUME MEASUREMENTS (dry)

⅛ teaspoon = 0.5 mL
¼ teaspoon = 1 mL
½ teaspoon = 2 mL
¾ teaspoon = 4 mL
1 teaspoon = 5 mL
1 tablespoon = 15 mL
2 tablespoons = 30 mL
¼ cup = 60 mL
⅓ cup = 75 mL
½ cup = 125 mL
⅔ cup = 150 mL
¾ cup = 175 mL
1 cup = 250 mL
2 cups = 1 pint = 500 mL
3 cups = 750 mL
4 cups = 1 quart = 1 L

VOLUME MEASUREMENTS (fluid)

1 fluid ounce (2 tablespoons) = 30 mL
4 fluid ounces (½ cup) = 125 mL
8 fluid ounces (1 cup) = 250 mL
12 fluid ounces (1½ cups) = 375 mL
16 fluid ounces (2 cups) = 500 mL

WEIGHTS (mass)

½ ounce = 15 g
1 ounce = 30 g
3 ounces = 90 g
4 ounces = 120 g
8 ounces = 225 g
10 ounces = 285 g
12 ounces = 360 g
16 ounces = 1 pound = 450 g

DIMENSIONS

1/16 inch = 2 mm
⅛ inch = 3 mm
¼ inch = 6 mm
½ inch = 1.5 cm
¾ inch = 2 cm
1 inch = 2.5 cm

OVEN TEMPERATURES

250°F = 120°C
275°F = 140°C
300°F = 150°C
325°F = 160°C
350°F = 180°C
375°F = 190°C
400°F = 200°C
425°F = 220°C
450°F = 230°C

BAKING PAN SIZES

Utensil	Size in Inches/Quarts	Metric Volume	Size in Centimeters
Baking or	8 × 8 × 2	2 L	20 × 20 × 5
Cake Pan	9 × 9 × 2	2.5 L	23 × 23 × 5
(square or	12 × 8 × 2	3 L	30 × 20 × 5
rectangular)	13 × 9 × 2	3.5 L	33 × 23 × 5
Loaf Pan	8 × 4 × 3	1.5 L	20 × 10 × 7
	9 × 5 × 3	2 L	23 × 13 × 7
Round Layer	8 × 1½	1.2 L	20 × 4
Cake Pan	9 × 1½	1.5 L	23 × 4
Pie Plate	8 × 1¼	750 mL	20 × 3
	9 × 1¼	1 L	23 × 3
Baking Dish	1 quart	1 L	—
or Casserole	1½ quart	1.5 L	—
	2 quart	2 L	—